Personnel Practice

Malcolm Martin BSc, MIMgt, FIPD is lead tutor for the Certificate in Personnel Practice programme at Manchester Open Learning, with responsibilities for design and delivery. He is a freelance trainer and consultant in human resource management. On graduating, he joined British Steel and subsequently moved to Dunlop, Guthrie, and the BBA Group, where he held managerial positions in industrial relations, project management, and personnel. He has directed numerous CPP courses, most being provided for corporate clients such as British Aerospace, Girobank, and Glasgow City Council. Malcolm lives in Lancashire.

Tricia Jackson BA, MSc (Personnel Management), Minst AM, FIPD is lead tutor in Employee Resourcing and a course leader for the Certificate in Personnel Practice at Manchester Open Learning. She is also a freelance training and personnel consultant, with a particular interest in representation at industrial tribunals. Tricia has many years' experience as a generalist practitioner in both the private (engineering and metallurgy) and public (local authority) sectors. More recently she held the post of senior lecturer at the Dearne Valley Business School, where she was involved in the design and delivery of their CPP programme. She has led numerous CPP courses on public open programmes and for the Northern Ireland Civil Service. Tricia lives in South Yorkshire.

฿

Other titles in the series:

Core Personnel and Development
Mick Marchington and Adrian Wilkinson

Employee Development
Rosemary Harrison

Employee Relations
John Gennard and Graham Judge

Employee Resourcing
Ted Johns and Stephen Taylor

Employee Reward
Michael Armstrong

The Institute of Personnel and Development is the leading publisher of books and reports for personnel and training professionals and students and for all those concerned with the effective management and development of people at work. For full details of all our titles please telephone the Publishing Department at IPD House on 0181 263 3387.

People and Organisations

Personnel Practice

Malcolm Martin
and
Tricia Jackson

Institute of Personnel and Development

Design by Curve

Typeset by Paperweight

Printed in Great Britain by
The Cromwell Press, Wiltshire

British Library Cataloguing in Publication Data
A catalogue record for this book is available from the British Library

ISBN 0-85292-678-2

The views expressed in this book are the authors' own and may not necessarily reflect those of the IPD.

INSTITUTE OF PERSONNEL
AND DEVELOPMENT

IPD House, Camp Road, London SW19 4UX
Tel.: 0181 971 9000   Fax: 0181 263 3333
Registered office as above. Registered Charity No. 1038333
A company limited by guarantee. Registered in England No. 2931892

Contents

Editors' foreword

People hold the key to more productive and efficient organisations. The way in which people are managed and developed at work has major effects upon quality, customer service, organisational flexibility and costs. Personnel and development practitioners can play a major role in creating the framework for this to happen, but ultimately they are dependent upon line managers and other employees for its delivery. It is important that personnel and development specialists gain the commitment of others and pursue professional and ethical practices that will bring about competitive success. There is also a need to evaluate the contribution that personnel and development approaches and processes make for organisational success, and to consider ways of making them more effective. Such an approach is relevant for all types of practitioner – personnel and development generalists and specialists, line managers, consultants and academics.

This is one of a series of books under the title *People and Organisations*. The series provides essential guidance and points of references for all those involved with people in organisations. It aims to provide the main body of knowledge and pointers to the required level of skills for personnel and development practitioners operating at a professional level in all types and sizes of organisation.

The series has been specially written to satisfy new professional standards defined by the Institute of Personnel and Development (IPD) in the United Kingdom and the Republic of Ireland and includes a volume designed for those seeking the Certificate in Personnel Practice (CPP), which often provides an access route into the professional scheme. The series also responds to a special need in the United Kingdom for texts structured to cover the knowledge aspects of new and revised National and Scottish Vocational Qualifications (N/SVQs) in Personnel and Training Development.

Three 'fields' of standards have to be satisfied in order to gain graduate membership of the IPD: (i) core management (ii) core personnel and development and (iii) any four from a range of more than 20 generalist and specialist electives. The three fields can be tackled in any order, or indeed all at the same time. A range of learning routes is available: full or part time educational course, flexible learning methods or direct experience. The standards may be assessed by educational and competence-based methods. The books in the series are suitable for supporting all methods of learning.

The series starts by addressing *core personnel and development* and four generalist electives: employee reward, employee resourcing, employee relations and employee development. Together, these cover the personnel and development knowledge requirements for graduateship of the IPD. These also cover the knowledge aspects of training and development and personnel N/SVQs at Level 4.

Core Personnel and Development by Mick Marchington and Adrian Wilkinson addresses the essential knowledge and understanding required of all personnel and development professionals, whether generalists or specialists. Practitioners need to be aware of the wide range of circumstances in which personnel and development processes take place and consequently the degree to which particular approaches and practices may be appropriate in specific circumstances. In addressing these matters, the book covers the core personnel and development standards of the IPD, as well as providing an essential grounding for human resource management options within business and management studies degrees. The authors are both well-known researchers in the field, working at one of the UK's leading management schools. Professor Marchington is also a chief examiner with the IPD.

Employee Reward by chief examiner Michael Armstrong has been written specially to provide extensive subject coverage for practitioners required by both the IPD's new generalist standards for employee reward and the personnel N/SVQ Level 4 unit covering employee reward. It is the first book on employee reward to be produced specifically for the purposes of aiding practitioners to gain accredited UK qualifications. *Employee Relations* by chief examiner Professor John Gennard and associate examiner Graham Judge explores the link between the corporate environment and the interests of the buyers and sellers of labour. It also demonstrates how employers (whether or not they recognise unions) can handle the core issues of bargaining, group problem-solving, redundancy, participation, discipline and grievances, and examines how to evaluate the latest management trends.

Employee Development by chief examiner Rosemary Harrison is a major new text, which extends the scope of her immensely popular earlier book of the same name to establish the role of human resource development (HRD) and its direction into the next century. After reviewing the historical roots of HRD, she considers its links with business imperatives, its national and international context, the management of the HRD function, and ways of aligning HRD with the organisation's performance management system. Finally, she provides a framework setting HRD in the context of organisational learning, the key capabilities of an enterprise and the generation of the new knowledge it needs.

Both these books, like Ted Johns and Stephen Taylor's *Employee Resourcing*, are carefully tailored to the new IPD and N/SVQ standards, while Malcolm Martin and Tricia Jackson's *Personnel Practice* is focused on the needs of those studying for the Certificate in Personnel Practice. This also gives a thorough grounding in the basics of personnel activities. The authors are experienced practitioners and lead tutors for one of the UK's main providers of IPD flexible learning programmes.

In drawing upon a team of distinguished and experienced writers and practitioners, the People and Organisations series aims to provide a range of up-to-date, practical texts indispensable to those pursuing IPD and N/SVQ qualifications in personnel and development. The books will also prove valuable to those who are taking other human resource management and employment relations courses, or who are simply seeking greater understanding in their work.

Mick Marchington   *Mike Oram*

List of abbreviations

ACAS	Advisory, Conciliation and Arbitration Service
CPD	Continuing Professional Development
CPP	Certificate in Personnel Practice
CRE	Commission for Racial Equality
ECJ	European Court of Justice
EOC	Equal Opportunities Commission
EU	European Union
GOQ	Genuine Occupational Qualification
HR	Human Resources
HRM	Human Resource Management
HSC	Health and Safety Commission
HSE	Health and Safety Executive
IIP	Investors in People
IMS	Institute of Manpower Studies
IPD	Institute of Personnel and Development
IPM	Institute of Personnel Management
IT	Information Technology
ITD	Institute of Training and Development
LEC	Local Enterprise Company
MbO	Management by Objectives
MIPD	Member of the Institute of Personnel and Development
NACEPD	National Advisory Council on Employment of People with Disabilities
NDC	National Disability Council
NVQ	National Vocational Qualification
NTA	National Training Award

PC   Personal Computer

PDP   Personal Development Plan

PMS   Performance Management System

PRP   Performance-Related Pay

SVQ   Scottish Vocational Qualification

TEC   Training and Enterprise Council

TUC   Trades Union Congress

Acknowledgements

Malcolm and Tricia would like to thank their respective partners, Christina and David, for their understanding and support during the completion of this book. Our thanks are also due to Sarah Mainwaring for her assistance with word processing this manuscript.

1 Introduction

OUR PURPOSE

The contents of this book follow the rationale set down in the Institute of Personnel and Development (IPD) Professional Standards for the Certificate in Personnel Practice (CPP). This programme is self-standing but also provides an access route to the professional scheme. CPP students, enrolled at an IPD-approved centre, will find that this book provides essential background reading to reinforce their learning.

The central purpose of the CPP is to develop competence in a range of core personnel and development skills together with the acquisition of underpinning knowledge and understanding. This book has been written to provide you, the reader, with a grounding in the basics of personnel activities. Thus it considers the breadth of knowledge and range of skills necessary for the effective performance of personnel work, while taking into account the organisational culture and environment.

Summaries of the structure and an overview of the contents of the book are provided in the sections following our coverage of the type of readers most likely to benefit from it and of the learning sources that you should use.

YOU, THE READER

The focus on the core skills required in managing and working effectively with people makes this book suitable for a large range of potential readers. The CPP programme is widely regarded as an ideal course for all newcomers to the profession but we expect that readers will belong to one or more of the following groups:

- personnel officers and managers who are newly appointed to the role but who lack previous generalist experience. (Further, you may be the sole personnel practitioner within your organisation, or your post may be a newly established one.)

- personnel assistants, administrators and secretaries who support more senior personnel staff

- staff who work in personnel-related areas, eg a personal assistant to a managing director or a payroll supervisor

- staff who work in specialist areas of personnel practice such as training, employee relations, or job evaluation who wish to progress into, or have more knowledge of, generalist roles

- line managers or supervisors who have responsibility for personnel activities

- owners or managers of small businesses who have overall responsibility for the 'people element' within them.

NB: We use the title 'personnel practitioners' throughout this book as a generic term to cover all of the above types of job and all levels of personnel work.

LEARNING SOURCES

This book has been written by two authors, both experienced in the field of personnel but with very different experiences, styles and, sometimes, perspectives. In order to understand each of the issues tackled within your own organisational circumstances, you will need to draw upon your own experience and perspective. To gain the maximum benefit from the book you will find it valuable to discuss the issues raised with appropriate people, particularly if you are relatively inexperienced in the areas under consideration. These people or 'learning sources' may include:

- senior colleagues, ie personnel specialists and line managers, peers, and subordinates who have knowledge and experience of the organisation and how it operates

- personnel managers and officers from sister, parent, and outside organisations

- specialists within your organisation such as company solicitors, health and safety officers, computer programmers/analysts, medical personnel, and occupational health advisers

- members of your local IPD branch and other networking bodies

- college tutors and fellow students

- employees of advisory bodies such as the Advisory, Conciliation and Arbitration Service (ACAS), the Health and Safety Executive (HSE), the Equal Opportunities Commission (EOC), and the Commission for Racial Equality (CRE).

You should establish contacts with these learning sources and make use of them to facilitate your learning experience. We shall be making periodic reference to your 'learning sources' throughout this book so, bearing in mind the above list, choose those sources that are going to be of most benefit to you in terms of their knowledge, availability, and willingness to help.

In addition to these 'people resources' there is also a range of publications available to assist you which provide general guidance and practical help. If you are a member of the IPD you should already have booklets on the following:

- the IPD Professional Standards

- IPD Continuing Professional Development (CPD)

- the IPD Codes of Practice (including the IPD Code of Professional Conduct), Guides and Key Facts.

ACAS has also produced a series of Advisory Booklets which provide invaluable assistance in a wide range of people management activities; you are highly recommended to acquire copies of these either for your personal use or for the whole of the personnel department.

Further, in order to keep up to date with changes in the world of personnel management, employment legislation, and case-law you should encourage your organisation to subscribe to a reputable information service such as that provided by Croner's. Subscriptions cover the initial reference material and a regular loose-leaf and electronic updating service. We would particularly recommend the *Reference Book for Employers* and the *Personnel Assistant's Handbook*, available from Croner Publications Ltd, Croner House, London Road, Kingston-upon-Thames, Surrey KT2 6SR.

THE STRUCTURE

This book has been designed to facilitate you, the reader, 'dipping in' to chapters and sections that are of particular interest. It is divided into nine chapters (including this one). The subject areas have been chosen to represent the major activities associated with personnel work, but there are obviously links between these activities, and these links are highlighted throughout. Brief details of the contents of each chapter are provided in the Overview section below.

The next two chapters help to set the scene for that which follows, ie the internal and external factors that exert an influence on an organisation are examined along with their effect on the work of personnel practitioners.

Each chapter contains the following features, where appropriate:

- an introduction
- an explanation why the topics covered are important to personnel practitioners
- the many and varied roles played by personnel practitioners
- a summary
- an activities section to encourage the acquisition of increased knowledge, the application of that knowledge in an organisational setting, and the planning of work experiences aimed at specific areas of skills development
- a section covering references, legislative acts and codes of practice, further reading, and recommended video titles.

The last two features highlight our desire to change your learning experience from a passive to an active one. You are recommended to tackle at least one activity from each chapter.

OVERVIEW

Chapter 1 – The introduction
As you will have seen, here we cover our purpose and the types of reader borne in mind when compiling this book, the wide range of learning sources available to you, and the structure and an overview of the contents of the book.

Chapter 2 – The role of the personnel practitioner

Consideration is given to the broader aspects surrounding the personnel function, as well as the wide range of activities involved in its execution. The differences between the terms 'personnel management' and 'human resource management' are examined, as well as the concepts of customer care and stakeholders. Finally, the effects of the internal corporate culture and the external corporate environment are summarised.

Chapter 3 – The legal background to personnel practice

Following on from Chapter 2's appreciation of the external factors acting upon the organisation, specific attention is now paid to the complex area of legislation. We concentrate on the employment law aspects and provide a summary of the relevant legislation under four main headings:

- civil law and, in particular, contracts of employment

- employment protection rights, concentrating on the important issues of unfair dismissal and equal opportunities

- other statutory legislation, covering the broad area of health and safety (data protection is covered in Chapter 8 – Personnel information systems)

- trade union law covering what trade unions are and their role in formulating collective agreements.

Our aim here is to provide general guidance on the basic knowledge requirements for personnel practitioners. We also seek to underline the difficulties of gaining a comprehensive knowledge and the need to seek expert advice when dealing with specific problems.

Chapter 4 – Recruitment and selection

Now we start the process of homing in on specific groups of personnel activities. Taking into account the legal setting, we consider the processes of:

- recruitment – ie job analysis (job descriptions and personnel specifications) and advertising

- selection – collecting information on candidates via application forms, interviews, tests etc, and assessing and comparing candidates (with specific guidance on good interviewing practice)

- induction – of new starters

- evaluation – of the whole process.

Chapter 5 – Training and development

In this chapter we look at definitions of training and development before working through the stages of the training cycle, starting with the identification of training needs through the stages of planning, implementing, and evaluating. Important issues such as the range of training and development techniques available are considered, as well as individuals' preferred learning styles. In addition, attention is paid to national training initiatives such as Investors in People and National Vocational Qualifications.

Chapter 6 – Discipline and grievance-handling

Disciplinary rules and grievance procedures are examined against the backdrop of relevant employment legislation. Tips on good practice in carrying out disciplinary and grievance interviews are given, along with broader guidance to highlight the need for your organisation to follow the correct procedures at all times. It is stressed that poor handling of disciplinary situations will increase the risk of claims to Industrial Tribunals of unfair dismissal and that employee relations problems may result from the mismanagement of formal grievances.

Chapter 7 – Performance management
First we examine the differences between performance appraisal and the broader concept of performance management. We make use of a practical example to stress the importance of ensuring that all performance management systems are closely integrated and directed towards achieving business goals. Performance appraisal is looked at in some detail: its purposes, motivational effects, history and trends, and the various components requiring consideration if one is designing a new scheme. Payment systems, particularly performance-related pay (PRP), are also covered, as are the legal considerations and the skills necessary to be an effective appraiser.

Chapter 8 – Personnel information systems
The reasons for and the importance of keeping accurate personnel records are emphasised here. Manual and computerised systems are considered (alongside the legal implications), with the concentration on the latter, ie the important role of computers, the many benefits they bring, and the large number of computer applications relevant to personnel work. Practical help is also provided for personnel practitioners called upon to computerise an existing personnel information system.

Chapter 9 – Personal effectiveness
This final chapter seeks to provide further guidance on the variety of skills necessary for effective performance in a personnel role. The broad issue of self-development is examined before more specific coverage is given of the following skills areas:

- communication – report writing and making presentations

- counselling – eg in handling redundancies, early retirements, sickness absence, personal problems

- negotiating, influencing, and persuading – in formal and informal situations

- time management – in and outside the workplace

- assertiveness – in work-related and personal situations.

Finally, you, the reader, are referred to the emphasis placed nowadays by a large number of professional associations such as the IPD on the concept of continuing professional development (CPD). The main focus of this concept is the proposition that learning and the acquisition of knowledge and skills are not a finite process but one that should carry on throughout our working lives. We have sought to reinforce this message, and hope that it is one you take to heart at this, the beginning, of a new learning experience.

2 The role of the personnel practitioner

INTRODUCTION

In this chapter we shall look at the role of personnel both in its traditional context and as a 'human resources' function. In doing so we shall also examine the concepts of 'customer care' and 'stakeholders'. Personnel management encompasses a huge variety of activities; and we shall look at the types of action that typify its role in the organisation.

Because the personnel function operates within an organisation we shall look briefly at the nature of organisations and at the relationships that personnel practitioners need to establish with managers, trade unions, and employees. The corporate environment is also important, and this includes the effect of changes that occur in that wider environment.

We believe that the personnel role is the most interesting and exciting one in any organisation. It may be a cliché that people are an organisation's greatest asset, but no organisation exists without them and nothing is achieved except through people. Therefore personnel practices go to the heart of the organisation and potentially have a role in every facet of its activities. As a personnel practitioner, you could conceivably be called on to help solve very personal individual problems. Equally, you could be asked to contribute to major strategic policy decisions in the boardroom. Quite possibly both could happen on the same day.

Because we consider it important for you to understand your role, each chapter will comment on the personnel practitioner's role in the context of the material covered by that chapter. Here, however, we are taking an overview.

PERSONNEL MANAGEMENT

Torrington and Hall (1991: 15) offer an excellent description of personnel management as it has traditionally been seen. For many small employers, and some larger ones, it will still be appropriate:

> Personnel Management is workforce-centred, directed mainly at the organisation's employees; finding and training them, arranging for them to be paid, explaining management's expectations, justifying management's actions, satisfying employees' work-related needs, dealing with their problems and seeking to modify management action that could produce unwelcome employee response... Although indisputably a management function, personnel is never totally identified with management interests, as it becomes ineffective when not able to understand and articulate the aspirations and views of the workforce.

It is worth splitting this quotation down, because it gives much pertinent information, although our interpretations should not be assumed to be exactly those that would be made by Torrington and Hall.

Finding employees

This is not just a question of advertising and recruiting, although this may be a major task. Effective practitioners build relationships with relevant local bodies such as schools, colleges, jobcentres, employment agencies, and the community at large. A good profile in the community helps to attract the best candidates. Finding employees is covered in detail in the chapter on recruitment and selection (Chapter 4).

Training employees

Occasionally this is a separate, or sister, function, but personnel and development are professionally linked. 'Training and development' does not mean only the arranging of training courses. As we shall see later, it can include diverse activities such as identifying needs, planning appropriate responses, and evaluating the success of these activities. It is important, for example, in the induction of employees to the organisation, in health and safety, and in helping an organisation to respond effectively to change.

Arranging payments

For many staff administrators in small organisations, administration of the payroll is their entry route into personnel practice. Paying employees regularly, properly, and on time is a contractual obligation backed up by legislation (the Employment Rights Act 1996 [ERA], for example). Proper authority, accuracy, and absolute meeting of deadlines are vital issues for payroll staff. Because of this, a payroll officer should be allowed to work to a regular routine and not be interrupted by other priorities. The demands of working in a personnel office can be slightly different – a point of which those making the transition from payroll to personnel need to be aware.

Personnel aspects of paying employees can, at one extreme, involve clarification of entitlement to individual pay items and, at the other, negotiating the pay rates themselves.

It is good practice (to reduce the possibility of fraud) for those who authorise payments (eg personnel practitioners) to have separate reporting relationships from those who pay employees (ie payroll staff).

Explaining management expectations

There is a wide range of issues where it is appropriate for a representative function in the organisation to explain management expectations. Personnel functions are usually the most appropriate, and can be expected to have the necessary communication skills. Where appropriate, they are likely to already work closely with trade unions or workplace representatives. Examples of issues which we have experience of explaining on behalf of our management teams are: productivity schemes, health and safety needs, and no-smoking policies.

A related area is collective agreements made between an organisation's management and a trade union (on behalf of members employed in that organisation). They determine terms and conditions that apply to the employment contract. Therefore they should be explained in co-operation with the trade union, and not left for shop stewards alone to explain.

Justifying management actions

Where you need to do this, we hope you will have been able to make a contribution to the decisions themselves. Justifying actions that you may not have chosen yourself is one of the greatest challenges for the personnel practitioner. It is a central aspect of managerial responsibility that, once you have put all your arguments, you accept and implement whatever is decided. That may be stressful, particularly if you have not been able to put those arguments at the right level. Typical actions that personnel practitioners might be called on to justify are: restructuring and redundancy, reductions in fringe benefits, changes within the place of work, and relocation.

Satisfying employees' work-related needs

These are issues such as health and safety, fringe benefits (company vehicles, for example), welfare matters, and long-term protection such as life assurance and pensions. In large companies some of these matters may be dealt with by a separate department.

Dealing with employees' problems

Grievances are raised on a huge range of issues. Many of these will be settled by line managers. Those issues that are not will invariably require a relatively 'neutral' broker – a personnel practitioner. We look at this in detail in the chapter on discipline and grievance-handling (Chapter 6).

Other employee problems for which you need to be prepared include early retirement, redundancy, debts, and bereavement.

Seeking to modify management's actions

An example of a management action may be a move from weekly to monthly pay. The simple modification of providing an interest-free loan may generate acceptability from employees and enable a senior manager to achieve his or her objectives. Personnel practitioners should be close to employees and be able to judge what will be acceptable to them. They should also recognise what may damage motivation and commitment, what may cause damaging stress, and what may lead to industrial action. The very high levels of stress being experienced by employees in the 1990s suggest there is a very serious challenge here. Unfortunately, personnel practitioners are not immune to stress themselves. They may be particularly vulnerable when they fail to modify those management actions that conflict with their own values. Confidence, assertiveness, judgement, and emotional resilience are qualities needed by effective practitioners. Given these qualities, practitioners are more likely to find that senior managers listen.

We shall look at how you can develop your personal skills in the chapter on personal effectiveness (Chapter 9).

Understanding and articulating employees' aspirations and views

The ability of personnel practitioners to influence management action depends on the ability to judge the outcomes of those actions. Judging outcomes means understanding the language of the employees; influencing managers means using the language managers understand. Understanding and communicating well with both employees and managers is an important skill for practitioners. You can foster both languages by spending time with each group.

Walking the floor is better than opening the door. Stay in your own office and you will meet only the more confident employees or those with specific issues to resolve, however wide your door may be open. Senior managers have their own language; that of the chief executive, for example, may be different from that of the board members. Management courses and finance for non-financial managers courses provide some of the vocabulary. You may be able to learn from social opportunities – talking to senior managers at in-company award ceremonies, for example. There may be external opportunities to learn the decision-makers' language by taking on a responsible community role – for example, becoming a school governor or a magistrate.

Employees at your establishment may be represented by trade unions. If so, that is another group with which to develop a good relationship. Our experience has been that those who become involved in trade unions are genuine and articulate people. Their influence can be valuable in resolving differences between employees and management. It is usually easier to resolve a matter with a few representatives than with a whole workforce. Nonetheless, in our view managers must always reserve the right to communicate directly with their own employees.

HUMAN RESOURCE MANAGEMENT

Your perception of human resource management (HRM) may be moulded by the organisation for which you work. Some see it simply as an alternative (either US or 'upmarket') term for personnel management but others note that it can conveniently encompass training and development, health and safety, pensions, and other major activities not regarded as pure 'personnel management' work. Sometimes there is a more strategic perception of human resources (HR): a view that it is a tougher, less people-sensitive function which is much closer to the decision-makers.

Torrington and Hall (1991: 15–16) provide us with another pertinent description:

> Human Resources Management is resource-centred, directed mainly at management needs for human resources (not necessarily employees') to be provided and deployed. Demand rather than supply is emphasised. There is greater emphasis on planning, monitoring and control, rather than mediation. Problem solving is with other members of management on human resource issues rather than directly with employees or their representatives. It is totally identified with management interests, being a general management activity, and is relatively distant from the workforce as a whole.

Thus there is a change in emphasis, so far as activities are concerned, and a clearer identification with 'management interests'. Perhaps those who adopt the title desire to avoid the marginal activities that can be 'dumped' on personnel practitioners. However, the core activities are not fundamentally different. For example, manpower-planning (anticipating the future employee needs of the business), a typical HR role, is also a personnel management activity. Pick up an HRM textbook and you will see activities that are found in personnel management textbooks too.

Small employers tend to recognise the term 'personnel management' but ignore 'human resource management' as being more appropriately associated with large organisations. It is interesting that the professional body, the Institute of Personnel and Development (IPD), chose not to include 'human resources' in its title following the merger between the Institute of Personnel Management and the Institute of Training and Development in July 1994.

So we are of the view that the distinction is not a particularly important one. Adoption of the title 'human resources' may gain some temporary advantage in senior management perceptions. This could be important, if it can be built upon. In any event, you will be judged on what you achieve for your employer, not by the title on your door.

How that judgement is made depends in large measure on the nature of your response to your employer's needs. In this context the next approach is helpful.

THE CUSTOMER CARE CONCEPT

This concept originated outside the personnel function. It is based on the idea that all functions have a responsibility to serve customers. Those functions that do not deal directly with the organisation's customers nevertheless have 'internal' customers. This concept applies a sound discipline to which it is easy to relate: we all experience the customer relationship when we are customers ourselves. In that position we expect to be treated with respect. Indeed, as people travel more, particularly to the USA and the Far East, they develop an understanding of what good customer care really means. In consequence, they also increase their own expectations.

Service-level agreements are an extension of the customer care concept so that it can operate within an organisation. A typical agreement might be one in which the personnel department agrees to fill all staff vacancies within, say, 10 weeks of authorisation. As practitioners, we have found that setting some standards of service goes down well with other functions and motivates us strongly to achieve them. For personnel departments (as with other functions and many professions) the question still arises: 'Who are our customers?' Are they other departments, prospective employees, current employees, senior managers, or all of these? Since the last option is essentially correct, how can we balance conflict between different customers – who will have priority?

One way of understanding the dilemma this poses is to look at the notion of stakeholders.

THE STAKEHOLDER CONCEPT

In the stakeholder concept these other parties or customers are seen as having a stake in our department's time. Although balancing conflicting interests may be seen as a managerial function, we all have to mediate between the various people who make demands on our time at and away from work.

As an example, consider others who have a stake in your personal time: your partner, your family, your source of income, any voluntary leisure commitments. You need continually to balance the demands of each of these on your time and energy and against each other.

Looking again at the work situation, the stakeholder concept is not restricted to internal departments. The organisation itself needs to consider a whole range of groups that have a stake in its activities. These are likely to include employees, shareholders, trade unions, the government, and local communities, as well as customers and suppliers.

Balancing the differing needs of stakeholders demands good communication, understanding, assertiveness, and judgement. It is a major challenge for all managers.

WHAT ARE YOU EXPECTED TO DO?

We have now looked at a number of personnel-related activities using the description adopted by Torrington and Hall (1991). Broad though our examination may be, it does not include every activity a personnel practitioner may be asked to do. You will probably identify activities with which you are involved that are only touched upon here, or even omitted altogether. Managing the company car fleet, editing the company newsletter, or carrying out health and safety audits are just three examples. Much of the work that falls to personnel departments may not be viewed as, strictly, personnel-related work. Indeed, management guru Peter Drucker has described the personnel department as the 'trash can' department taking on almost any activity that no one else wanted!

It is important to find the balance between customer care activities, when you try to 'delight' customers, and taking on 'trash-can' activities, which will not earn any 'brownie points'. The latter are activities that waste your time and do not gain any credit from the people who have influence over your career. Identifying which is which is not always easy, but it is not possible to please all the people all the time; priorities have to be set. You may want to keep an eye on what activities influential people regard as being most important.

There is an increasing view that many personnel activities should be done by line managers, leaving time for personnel practitioners to concentrate on the medium- to long-term strategic issues. At a recent Certificate in Personnel Practice course one of our guest speakers put it succinctly: 'We must avoid being embroiled in detailed reactive issues; in essence, more day-to-day personnel activities must be the responsibility of line management.'

WHAT ACTIONS CAN PRACTITIONERS TAKE?

We describe several types of action below. In practice, the type of things that you can do arise from a complex mix of the authority vested in you, your persuasive abilities, your credibility with decision-makers, your responsibilities, and the norms of your organisation. To these you should add your own capabilities, risk tolerance, emotional resilience, and assertiveness.

Generally, you will have to discover most of the organisational factors in the mix for yourself. Observing and taking counsel from your boss, others in your department, and others in the organisation is the usual way. Personal effectiveness can be increased though self-development, as we outline later.

However, if you are a newly established 'personnel person' within your organisation you will have less advice to draw upon. If you have grown to the position from within the organisation you will already have some idea of the authority you have and your own credibility. If newly appointed, then your manager will probably indicate the boundaries within which you can act. All being well, you will have a job description setting out your main responsibilities and accountabilities (we look at job descriptions in Chapter 4). This job description may indicate your 'authority'; perhaps it specifies a budget, but it is unlikely to be specific about every activity that you will undertake.

One approach is to examine each activity and in each case ask: 'Should I be taking administrative action, advisory action, or executive action?' The answer will lie in the factors we discussed above. Let's have a look at each type of action.

Administrative action

This consists of maintaining procedures and operating systems. For example, a personnel practitioner may be advised of the outcome of salary negotiations and then be expected to calculate new salaries and notify the payroll department. Other examples are the headcount (regularly establishing the number of employees), recruitment activities, maternity leave, and issuing letters of appointment. In the case of administrative activities you will usually be given some specific instructions initially and, if supervised, details of how to carry out the task.

Advisory action

This assumes you have some specialist knowledge or information and can provide guidelines for managerial decisions. Areas in which personnel practitioners typically advise are disciplinary procedures and employment law. Clear knowledge and understanding here will enhance your credibility considerably. Keep in mind, though, that this is a difficult area and do seek advice yourself, perhaps from more senior colleagues or the Advisory, Conciliation and Arbitration Service (ACAS), if in any doubt.

In salary negotiations personnel practitioners frequently brief the negotiating team on current remuneration packages or on market rates. They may also be members of the negotiating team.

Executive action

This means taking full responsibility for certain tasks, making decisions, and taking appropriate action. For example, in some organisations a personnel practitioner may be sufficiently senior, and authorised, to take the decision to dismiss an employee. Similarly, some practitioners take full responsibility for salary negotiations, ie for reaching an agreement and implementing it. You will not, of course, be taking such decisions unless you have been very clearly authorised to do so.

To increase your understanding of these different types of action we suggest you try the appropriate exercise at the end of this chapter.

CORPORATE CULTURE

As we said earlier, personnel activities take place within an organisation. This means that your role, what you do, and how you do it are inevitably influenced, or even constrained, by its nature or corporate culture.

It is valuable to understand your organisation: it will help you decide how to earn those 'brownie points' that we mentioned earlier. It may be that you do not want to advance your career in terms of responsibility. But identifying and performing well in those activities that are valued will enhance your esteem, influence and, perhaps, your salary.

If you have changed employers during your working life then you will appreciate how they differ even within the same industry sector. The differences between large and small organisations, between the various industry sectors, and between public and private are even more marked.

Don't assume that the ways in which tasks are carried out in your organisation, say the way in which job descriptions are prepared, is the only approach or indeed a necessary approach. Many companies, for example, survive profitably without job descriptions.

Within your organisation, observe the characteristics or 'culture' of different departments. In our experience, sales teams are often characterised by positive, outgoing attitudes and a preoccupation with status, targets, performance, and reward (eg the commission scheme). Production teams

---

The nature of reporting relationships
Does everyone have one established manager or do managers change frequently in response to business needs?

The management style
Are employees managed by instruction and control or by consultation and personal development?

Pay
Is it fixed or linked to performance, grading, or 'merit'?

Employees
Are they valued? If so, how is this obvious?

Customer care
Are customers valued? If so, how is it obvious?

Costs
Do they matter? How does their importance compare with potential income?

Profit
Are employees conscious of profit? Is it relevant or important?

Business objectives
Do employees identify with business objectives?

Status symbols
What role do they play? Are they a substitute for power or remuneration?

Ethics
Are ethics important? If so, how is it obvious?

Risks
What are the consequences of making a mistake?

There is a series of indicators to show whether an organisation has a positive or negative culture (see the activities at the end of this chapter).

are more likely to evidence a 'no-nonsense' attitude, be driven by meeting deadlines, and reject what they see as 'time-wasting' activities (such as writing job descriptions, perhaps).

The predominant corporate culture will depend on the nature of its business. A trading company is likely to be driven by sales attitudes. A manufacturing company is more likely to be characterised by production attitudes. There are many ways of identifying and describing corporate culture. The boxed text on page 13 gives examples of some other differences that characterise culture.

CORPORATE ENVIRONMENT

We do not need to look far to see tremendous change in our society. Indeed, change is becoming the third great certainty (the other two being death and taxes!). Look back over the last 10 years. How many public bodies have been privatised, how many turned into agencies? Reflect on education and health where business thinking (local management of schools, purchaser–supplier relationships, GP fund-holding) has been injected into non-business organisations. Look at the effects of European legislation. Changes in the pension age and new rights for part-time employees are just two effects in the employment area alone. How many employees experienced redundancy in the early 1990s? Have you heard of the 'leaner', 'flatter' organisation? To what extent have 'green' issues come to the fore?

The environment in which organisations operate is wide, and change originates from six areas which may be summarised with the mnemonic PESTLE. The areas are shown below:

- *political*: changes brought about by powerful bodies such as governments, the European Union (EU), the trade union movement, and regulatory bodies

- *economic*: economic prosperity; interest rates (that affect the cost of borrowing and, potentially, company profitability); unemployment; demand for goods; import tariffs

- *social*: one-parent families; an ageing population; consumer expectations; demographic changes (changes in the structure of the population); lifestyles; lobby groups

- *technological*: developments in medicine; computers; energy sources

- *legal*: new laws originating from Acts of Parliament; interpretations of the law by courts; the EU and European courts; international laws (eg fishing quotas)

- *environmental*: climatic change; acid rain; pollution; consumer attitudes to these issues

The sources of change are often interrelated. For example, equal opportunities for women (a legal change) was spurred on by social change (women's liberation).

Peter Wickens, while still personnel director for Nissan, expressed it succinctly for us at a meeting of the former IPM: 'Change is inevitable – in a progressive organisation change is constant.'

Managers should anticipate and respond to the effects that such changes have on their organisations if the latter are to remain viable. Training is often an important response, so we shall look at these areas again in more detail in Chapter 5.

There are some serious implications arising from the changing environment for employees. Flatter organisations mean fewer opportunities for promotion. Thus promotion can be less easily used to increase earnings or as a reward. Less security implies that employees will seek opportunities to develop and grow to ensure they have marketable skills and experience to help them if they need to change employers. They will want experience in activities that are in demand so that they have relevant achievements to put on their CVs.

To be effective in this changing world, you as personnel practitioners need to keep in close touch with your corporate environment, with employees, and with the community at large. Doing so will help you to anticipate and respond effectively to people issues. Reading the IPD's magazine, *People Management*, and keeping in touch with current affairs is important. Similarly, building good links between yourself, your management team, employees, and the community is also an important task. How will you do it?

BUILDING BRIDGES

Spend some time considering the questions below and the discussion that follows each; they should give you some clues as to how you can develop the links we have just mentioned.

- How do employees make contact with you? Interruptions are a major source of inefficiency but, at the same time, you cannot afford to be remote. Is your department close to where most employees work? Is your department found easily? An open door encourages contact, whereas a formal appointment system may discourage it. For a larger department a 'front desk' helps avoid the whole department's being interrupted by an enquiry.

- How do you make contact with employees? Making time to 'walk the floor' can ensure employees know who you are, foster contact, and help you to assess the general mood or change in mood. It takes time, of course, on your part and on that of employees. Furthermore, not all management teams will welcome direct contacts between you and (their) employees in this way. Another approach is to make a habit of going to see employees directly to deal with matters, rather than telephoning, calling them to your office, or issuing a memo. You can inform the employee's manager first, if protocol requires it.

- How good are your relationships with trade union representatives? Keeping representatives in touch with issues which concern their members helps build good relationships. You need to be careful what you do discuss, consulting senior management members first if you have any doubts. Nevertheless, making time to talk with the representatives and taking an interest in their viewpoint can be revealing, and you may very probably see your organisation in a different light. Often you will pick up minor issues which you can remedy or more serious ones in which you can still have an influence.

- Are you in touch with your management team? Using a telephone is efficient and promotes good time management. On the other hand, visiting individuals may be more effective and, crucially, builds relationships. Be mindful of people's time and the pressures on them; nonetheless, most managers enjoy discussing issues face to face. A useful tip is to stand up for informal meetings, thus encouraging contact to be short. The tip also works for telephone calls, because your voice changes when you stand up – it conveys more urgency. Attend relevant formal meetings. Some organisations have a 'meetings' culture, in which case you will probably want to attend as few as possible. Whatever the culture, try to be present at important meetings and go along prepared to make a positive contribution.

- Does the community regard your organisation as a good employer? The manner in which you recruit, respond to unsolicited applications, and reject unsuccessful job applicants is often commented upon, especially if you are in a small community. Contact with the community from a major employer invariably increases the regard in which that employer is held. It may also provide you with valuable information; and liaison between personnel practitioners and local bodies, such as schools or societies, is usually welcomed. If community activities interest you, then you may be able to foster links in the community by being active in, for example, the Chambers of Commerce, or in the various clubs for executive, professional, and business people.

- What is the department's profile? The quality of communications can help set the scene. Here we are thinking of examples such as induction information and the staff handbook, notices on the notice boards, clarity of payslips, notification of pay increases, and contributions to the company newsletter. How you deal with personal issues will go deeper. Learning good counselling skills helps here. Actions always speak louder than words.

- How will you react to a redundancy programme? Redundancy-handling is one of the most emotive issues with which you are likely to come into contact. We assume that this will be guided by experienced people in your organisation, and therefore it is not dealt with in any great detail in this book. Nonetheless you will probably be identified with such programmes by other employees, and you should think through the implications of this. If you do need to handle a redundancy exercise without support from more senior personnel, then we recommend you talk to your local ACAS official as early as possible.

- What else may you have to face? Other personal issues such as bereavements, maternity, AIDS, debts, or bankruptcy may well demand your attention. The sympathetic and practical way in which you handle these will reflect strongly on your department's reputation. Like redundancy, it helps if you think through in advance how you will handle such issues.

You will find help and guidance on developing the skills necessary in Chapter 9.

SUMMARY

Personnel practice and management offer an interesting and exciting career. Potentially the function encompasses any issue in which the employer, as a corporate body, relates to the employee. Therefore you should have a good relationship both with employees (and their representatives – usually a trade union – where applicable) and managers at all levels, as well as relevant outside bodies.

The personnel function provides a service to the operational functions. It is not in itself profit-earning or a direct contributor to the operational purpose. What it does is to assist others in that role. To be effective it needs to be mindful of caring for its 'customers' and of the various stakeholders, who may have conflicting interests.

The actions that personnel practitioners can take invariably include administrative actions, and frequently they include advisory actions. In many cases, particularly at senior levels, practitioners may have authority to take executive decisions as well. For practitioners to be well regarded they need to be in tune with the corporate culture in which they work: they need to identify what is valued.

In the 1990s practitioners cannot ignore the pace of change and the effects that that has on employers and employees. Anticipating these effects will greatly enhance your performance.

To be well informed, practitioners need to build and maintain good relationships with a variety of stakeholders, particularly managers, trade unions, employees, and the community from which their employees come.

ACTIVITIES

1 Study the table on activities (Table 1 on page 18). Identify activities and tasks that take place in your personnel department.

   • Now identify the types of action that your department takes, placing a tick in the appropriate column(s).

   • Circle those particular actions that you might take yourself.

   • Discuss the results with others in a similar position in different organisations.

   • How do the activities of your department differ from theirs?

2 If you are a personnel or training practitioner, prepare a 30-word statement describing the purpose of your job. (If you are not yet in the function then speculate on the purpose of someone who is in such a position in your organisation.) Ask yourself:

   • Why do I have a job?

   • What would happen if the tasks I do were not completed?

   • How might my contribution be measured?

   • How might my performance be measured?

3 Think about other departments such as purchasing, finance, research and development, marketing, and data processing, as well as the

personnel department. What characterises people in those departments in terms of attitudes to, and concern with, the following issues: deadlines, accuracy, documentation, cost, profit, status, ethics, and personal financial reward?

4 Reflect on your employer and another employer with whom you are reasonably familiar, perhaps your mother or father's or your partner's employer. Make a list of the differences in attitude and concerns as outlined in 3 above and any other differences that are appropriate. How do you account for the differences?

5 Taking your organisation, or the site within it where you work, identify the main stakeholders. Which groups or organisations benefit from the existence of your employer? Who would lose if it became less successful or reduced its presence? What implications do these stakeholders have for your work? (As an example, in a small community, the local school may be a major supplier of new employees. The implications for you could be that you would wish to foster good relations with the school.)

Table 1 Activities and tasks of personnel departments

Activity	Task	Executive	Advisory	Admin.
Recruitment and selection	Determining methods Defining requirements Advertising Processing applications Interviewing Taking part in decisions Organising programmes Offering jobs Taking up references			
Industrial relations	Attending meetings Applying agreements Acting as a specialist Advising on law Participating in procedures			
Direction and policy	Developing policy External relations			
Health, safety and welfare	Counselling Occupational health Pensions			
Pay administration	Instructions to pay Initiate transactions Dealing with complaints			
Manpower – planning and control	Maintaining records Controlling numbers			
Training and development	Identifying needs Providing training			
Employee communications	Planning Operating			
Organisation design	Job descriptions			
Information and records	Determining needs Providing information			

Adapted from Farnham (1990: 114).

6 Look at the positive and negative indicators shown in Table 2 below. How does your employer compare with the examples given? Is there a positive or negative culture prevailing? Look back at the section on 'Building bridges'. Are there any actions you can take that would increase a positive perspective, particularly in the relationship between personnel practitioners, employees, their representatives, and the management team?

Table 2 Positive and negative indicators of corporate culture

Aspect	Positive indicators	Negative indicators
Organisational and personal pride	'Company problems are our problems'	'What do I care – I only work here'
Performance/excellence	A success orientation	'It's good enough'
Teamwork/communication	Communication is open and two-way	Destructive conflict and unnecessary competition
Leadership and supervision	Leaders and supervisors are concerned with people and productivity	Leaders and supervisors see their role as checking and policing subordinates
Profitability and cost-effectiveness	People see a connection between profits and their well-being as employees	Opportunities for cost savings and increased sales are neglected or overlooked
Relationships with colleagues	People work hard to see that all colleagues are treated with dignity and respect	Company and employees tend to look at each other as having separate interests
Customer and consumer relations	Customer satisfaction is seen as vital to personal and organisational success	The customer and consumer tend to be looked upon as a kind of unavoidable burden
Honesty and safety	Safety regulations are taken seriously; people place a high value on integrity and support integrity in others	People are careless with company money or products, and neglectful in following or enforcing safety practices
Training and development	Training and development are looked upon as an integral part of all that occurs within the organisation	Training is seen as unimportant and barely related to the day-to-day work
Motivation and change	People are eager to consider new and innovative approaches	People look at new ways of doing things with unwarranted suspicion or mistrust

Based on work by Allen and Pilnick and adapted from Edwards (1988).

REFERENCES AND FURTHER READING

BEARDWELL I. *and* HOLDEN L. (1994) *Human resource management*. London, Pitman Publishing.

EDWARDS E. (1988) 'Corporate culture'. *Management Accounting*. May. p19.

FARNHAM D. (1990) *Personnel in context*. 3rd ed. London, Institute of Personnel Management.

HACKETT P. (1991) *Personnel: the department at work*. London, Institute of Personnel Management.

TORRINGTON D. *and* HALL L. (1991) *Personnel management: a new approach*. Hemel Hempstead, Prentice Hall.

WEIGHTMAN J. (1993) *Managing human resources*. 2nd ed. London, Institute of Personnel Management.

3 The legal background to personnel practice

WHY IS IT IMPORTANT?

Many personnel practitioners and line managers feel that bringing the law into employment relationships creates rigidity and sometimes makes it difficult for the business to respond to opportunities. Employees, on the other hand, often feel that the law provides a degree of protection from poor management and exploitation. Many other feelings surround the question of law and employment. Some may arise from political beliefs, others from personal experience. The extent to which strong feelings exist, and their relevance to personnel practice, varies from organisation to organisation. Government organisations necessarily attach great importance to legal matters, whereas some entrepreneurial businesspeople may seek to minimise, or try to disregard, the impact of the law on their employment practices. Other employers adopt employment practices that are in excess of any minimum provided by the law. They aspire to practices that are the best that can be found, embracing the spirit as well as the letter of the law. One example, in the equal opportunities area, is the development of a truly diverse workforce in which every employee's dignity is genuinely respected.

Whatever an employer's intentions are, it is likely that there will be times when an employee feels that he or she has been unfairly treated. If that employee believes that the employer has acted unlawfully, then he or she may make a claim to an industrial tribunal. If the tribunal upholds the claim it will, in most cases, award compensation. Such compensation may be thousands of pounds or, in some types of claim, an unlimited amount. Whether the claim is upheld or not, substantial preparation work is involved if the employer decides to fight the claim. Such work makes no direct contribution to business objectives, and adverse publicity may even damage achievement of those objectives. In some cases, trade unions can challenge the employing organisation by taking actions that disrupt its activities, damage its relationship with customers, and threaten its profitability. Therefore a knowledge of employment law is a key requirement for personnel practitioners.

However, employment law is not an area where issues are necessarily clear cut. Indeed, even at an industrial tribunal with a legally qualified chairman, one party involved may not agree that the law has been correctly interpreted and may appeal against the decision reached. The matter will then be referred to a higher court for them to advise on interpretation of the law.

In some cases it falls to the House of Lords to decide this. One consequence is that, quite frequently, the precise way in which the law is interpreted changes.

So, although we shall explain the basic principles that you need to know, you are likely also to need advice from more senior colleagues, the Advisory, Conciliation and Arbitration Service (ACAS) (see later in this chapter), or legal specialists.

EMPLOYMENT LEGISLATION

It is useful to see employment legislation in four groups: civil law, employment protection rights, other statutory legislation, and trade unions.

Civil law

This group deals with relations between two parties. Contracts are an example; breaches of them entitle one party to sue the other (litigation). Typically, in employment, this would be for failure to give proper notice (an example of wrongful dismissal). Until recently, breaches of employment contracts would be dealt with at a County Court. Now, most breach of employment contract claims may be heard by industrial tribunals.

Another example of civil law is the duty of care. This is implicit in all employment contracts. So an employee may sue his or her employers for damages if, for example, he or she is injured at work and believes the employer to be responsible. In doing so the employee may cite breaches of regulations – for example, not being informed of safety procedures. Personal injury claims are currently a matter for the County Court.

Employment protection rights

The major employee right is the right not to be unfairly dismissed, and this applies irrespective of the employee's hours of work. At the time of writing (April 1997), the length of service an employee requires before acquiring these rights is two years. This may change, which only emphasises the need to read relevant magazines or consult reference books to keep up to date. The other main area of protection is the right not to be discriminated against. This comprises laws that protect equal opportunities, covering such areas as maternity rights and equal pay, reasonable adjustments for the disabled, and the employment of ex-offenders. Redress in employment protection matters is sought by a claim to an industrial tribunal. The onus is on the aggrieved party to make this claim. This body of employment protection legislation is a major area for employers and one with which personnel practitioners need to be familiar.

Other statutory legislation

Many obligations are placed on the employer by other statutory legislation. In contrast to civil law and the employment protection legislation (where claims are made for damages or compensation) many breaches in this area leave employers (principally directors, but also managers and in some cases employees) open to criminal prosecution, fines and (in some extreme cases) imprisonment. In Northern Ireland, such legislation includes the question of religious discrimination.

The Health and Safety at Work Act 1974 (HASWA) and the Control of Substances Hazardous to Health Regulations 1994 (COSHH) are another two highly important pieces of legislation. (A further one, in the employment arena, is the Data Protection Act 1984, which we shall look at in Chapter 8.) Health and safety is a major area of legislation, especially for employers in the industrial sector, and one with which those who have health and safety responsibilities must obviously be familiar.

Trade unions

The legislation that regulates activities of trade unions is complex and we shall touch on the main issues only. But understanding how trade unions fit into the employment framework is important for personnel practitioners. They need to know what a trade union is, what shop stewards are, understand the significance of collective agreements, and be aware of the power of trade unions as manifested in the threat of industrial action. Awareness of ACAS and the services it offers is also important (see page 42).

We shall look at the key issues in each area, starting with civil law.

CIVIL LAW

What is a legal contract?

When one person agrees to do something for another a contract exists. It may be binding in honour only, as for example when we offer to buy a drink for a friend (and he or she accepts our offer). In this example, if we suddenly discover we have left our money at home (and therefore cannot fulfil the contract), we do not expect to be sued! Nonetheless, an informal contract was made and, in failing to fulfil it, we would have broken that contract.

Legal contracts are more binding and, if we break them, the other party is entitled to damages. A failure to agree on what damages are due entitles the aggrieved party to seek redress in a Civil Court or, if it is an employment contract, in an industrial tribunal. Legal contracts can be made by people or by 'legal entities' such as a limited company.

An employment contract is a particular type of legal contract. But let's first look at the conditions needed for a legal contract to exist.

- *Agreement*   An offer has to be made and accepted. You might offer to buy someone's car for £5,000, but no agreement is reached until the offer is accepted. In employment, offers are often 'subject to' issues such as references, a medical, or verification of qualifications. In such cases, agreement is not reached until all the 'subject to' issues have been resolved.

- *Consideration*   There has to be an exchange of benefits – the car in return for your £5,000, for example. In employment it could be wages in return for work. 'Voluntary work' can be a grey area but, unless something tangible is given in return (accommodation perhaps), there will be no legal contract.

- *Intention*   Both parties must intend to form a legally binding contract. This may be presumed, as in employment contracts, or should be recorded in writing, as in agreements between friends and relatives. Buying cars from friends can be problematic. If your friend gets a better offer while you are at the building society, it may be legally, as well as practically, difficult to enforce the contract. For self-employed people, employing friends and relatives can be problematic unless a specific legal contract is made.

- *Certainty* It has to be clear what the parties have agreed so that the contract can be established with certainty. Oral agreements, though having the status of legal contracts if clearly made, can be difficult to enforce. If it proves difficult to establish with certainty what was agreed, then the contract may be void. For this reason it is good practice to put employment contracts into writing.

- *Consent* The parties must come together freely and not under duress. In practice, unemployed people will often feel under pressure and can easily agree to terms they dislike. Unfortunately such 'duress' is regarded as a normal fact of life. It does not invalidate the contract.

- *Legality* Contracts can be formed for legal purposes only. This has implications for illegal activities, such as drug dealing. In instances where disputes cannot be resolved by recourse to law, they are often settled by use of violence.

- *Capacity* The person making the contract on behalf of an organisation must be properly authorised to do so. This is very important for you as a personnel practitioner. If you offer an employment contract without proper authority, your organisation could disown the decision. This would place you in a most invidious position and almost certainly leave you liable to disciplinary action. If the rejected employee had already accepted your offer, and handed in notice in his or her current employment, he or she may seek damages.

Notice that contracts do not have to be in writing. Many offers are made and accepted over the telephone. If it can be established that the above conditions have been met, then a legal contract exists. Telephone offers are quicker and therefore reduce the danger of losing a good candidate while a written contract is being prepared. They can make negotiations easier so long as both parties are prepared for them and you have clear authority to reach an agreement. In the longer term, written offers and acceptance have the advantage that both parties know exactly what has been agreed. Therefore there is less room for confusion (if references prove to be unsatisfactory, for example).

You need to find out whether your organisation has a policy on how offers should be made, or whether you are expected to make use of your best judgement.

Offers made by post may be accepted by post. Offers can also be accepted by a person's behaviour: for example, arriving for work would betoken acceptance. It may be helpful to place a time limit on an offer, or formally to withdraw it if it is not accepted within a satisfactory time-scale.

What is an employment contract?

It is important to understand when someone who is doing work for you is an employee and when he or she is a self-employed contractor.

You may wish to offer work to a person who claims to be self-employed. One difficulty, if you reach an agreement on that basis, is that the Inland Revenue may not be willing to treat that person as self-employed. In that case you, the employer, will probably have to pay tax and National Insurance contributions to the Inland Revenue for the person (even if he or she has already been paid without deductions).

On the other hand, if a person is an *employee*, then he or she has a wide range of employment rights, including the right not to be unfairly dismissed. The claim to be an employee could come after a contract has ended, in order to assert employment rights.

So, let's have a look at the distinction.

If you have your house decorated you do not, usually, employ a decorator; what you do is make a contract for service. However, if your organisation retains a decorator to decorate its premises, then that person could be its employee. If so, the organisation would then have a contract of service.

Employees are people who do the work for you, or your organisation, personally (ie they cannot subcontract the work to others), are supervised, and work specified hours. They are paid on a scale used for employees and pay tax by PAYE. They have a contract of employment and receive other benefits such as sick pay and holidays. Employees have employment rights, including an entitlement to written particulars of employment.

Self-employed people usually provide their own equipment (such as paintbrushes in the case of decorators) and will usually work for others as well as your organisation. They submit invoices and may be VAT-registered. They may contract to do a particular task (as opposed to working set daily hours), and any profit or loss in doing the work accrues to the person rather than the organisation. So as not to be held liable for any tax or National Insurance contributions, anyone contracting work from the self-employed may be wise to see a supporting letter from the Inland Revenue or a contractor's certificate.

If self-employed people do work for you, make sure this second set of conditions is satisfied. If in doubt, you are usually safer to employ them on a contract of employment, deduct tax under PAYE, and accept that they will have employment rights. If you choose not to do so, you could find yourself liable for their tax and, when ending the contract, discover they are claiming employment rights nevertheless.

If contract of employment is made, remember that a statement of written particulars should be provided within two months.

Contracts of employment

The contract sets out the legal basis of the relationship. Therefore it should include those matters on which you wish your employee to be legally bound and matters on which you, as an employer, will be legally bound. For example, you may want legally to bind an employee to your office hours. If there is a clear written agreement specifying this as part of the contract, then the hours become contractual.

Typically, disciplinary procedures are not part of the contract and it is advisable if only the minimum details required are referred to in the written particulars. You may have good reason to use judgement in operating disciplinary procedures. If such procedures are contractual, then a failure to follow them to the letter can result in a breach of contract claim.

It is important to remember that contracts cannot be changed unilaterally. To change a contract, both parties have to agree.

It is impossible to predict every possible employment situation that can arise. Therefore in areas where judgement or discretion is needed some matters as far as possible should not be contractual. Typical examples might be bonus scheme rules, job descriptions, and procedures. For the employer, deciding the degree of flexibility that should exist in the employment relationship is an important decision and requires careful judgement, although the final decision whether a particular term is contractual or not may rest with the courts.

Just to clarify the issue further, let's take the example of job descriptions. If you include a job description in an employment contract, then every variation in the duties of the job can, potentially, become a legal issue. For this reason it is advisable to include only the job title in the contract (indeed technically even this could be left for the written particulars). Similarly there is no requirement to include a job description in the written particulars, only a job title. Indeed, there is no legal need to have a job description at all.

The degree of formality involved in job descriptions affects an employer's flexibility to a significant degree. At one extreme, a lot of formality (job descriptions signed, or included in the contract) tends to encourage disputes over duties. Such disputes can focus on wording rather than the purpose of the job or the interests of the parties concerned. At the other extreme, complete informality (no job descriptions) may aid early resolution but can make it much more difficult if relationships do eventually break down. In informal situations it is easy for the employer to have one expectation about the employee's responsibilities and for the employee to have another.

Certain matters are implicit in an employment contract and are not usually written down. They apply whether the parties specifically agree to include them or not. They are:

- statutory requirements (such as those in the HASWA)

- common law duties (such the duty of care and co-operation with the employer)

- custom and practice (such as tea breaks, in cases where they are established).

Other matters that are clearly agreed between the two parties are explicit parts of the contract. If you want a matter to be contractual you need to be very careful in drawing up the contract, because it will not be easy to vary it later. For example, the place of work is usually part of the contract, so state it clearly and accurately.

However, you can put into the contract reasonable rights to vary aspects of the contract. So, in the case of the place of work, you might include a mobility clause. Indeed, you can put into the contract (and written particulars) variation clauses for any right that you may wish to vary, so long as the variation is justifiable and reasonable; but if you are providing for something that might happen some time in the future, you should still consult the employee(s) concerned when the variation is required.

Finally, it is important to include the notice period for termination of the contract by either party. Alternatively, the statutory minimum notice periods (based on length of service) may be stated.

Written particulars
Written particulars represent the employer's view of the terms of the relationship; where they conflict with contractual terms, the contract will prevail. Since 1978 it has been intended that employees should be entitled to know specific details about their terms and conditions of employment in a written statement. This right was strengthened by legislation in 1993; for example, the time within which a statement is to be produced was reduced from 13 weeks to two months. New employees now have this right to written particulars of their employment after one month's employment. Today these rights are provided for in the Employment Rights Act 1996 (ERA).

Look at the boxed text on page 28 that describes the required content of written particulars. Think through why the law provides these rights and what benefits they confer.

• Is it fair and reasonable for employees to know where they stand?

• Do written particulars protect employees from maltreatment? If so, how?

• Is a better understanding between employer and employee likely to arise as a result of putting particulars in writing?

• Why do you think many employers still do not provide written particulars? Is it:

   • through lack of knowledge of the law?

   • to save administration costs?

   • for power, gained by keeping employees ignorant of their rights?

Compiling written particulars demands care. Simplicity can give rise to anomalies because simple solutions do not recognise different sets of circumstances. An example of this might be an employer who gives 25 days holiday a year plus all public and bank holidays. This is a simple rule, but how do you interpret it for an employee who works only Monday and Tuesday each week? You could 'pro-rata' the 25 days to 10, but how do you handle public and bank holidays, which often fall on a Monday?

On the other hand, complex systems can lead to confusion and often mistrust. For example, a system could be devised where we add up how many holidays have been taken and then pay the part-time employee for only some of them. Of the 25 days' holiday plus the 8 public and bank holidays we might pay 13.2 days (2/5ths of 33 days) as one day per month plus one every 10 months. The employee could accumulate payable time at that rate and be paid the amount of entitlement that they had accumulated when they took a holiday. Such a scheme might be precisely

---

Written particulars

The following are required in one document, termed 'The Principal Statement':

- names of employer and employee

- date when employment began

- date when continuous employment began

- scale or rate of remuneration or method of calculation

- intervals at which remuneration is paid

- terms and conditions relating to hours of work (including normal working hours)

- holiday entitlement (including any entitlement to accrue holiday pay)

- job title or brief job description

- place of work.

The following may be provided in separate documents:

- terms relating to injury, sickness, and sick pay

- pensions and pension schemes

- period of notice each party must give to terminate the contract

- where the employment is temporary, how long it is likely to last, or the termination date for a fixed-term contract

- collective agreements which directly affect terms and conditions

- disciplinary rules and steps in the disciplinary and grievance procedures, specifying the people with whom, and how, an employee can raise a grievance or apply if dissatisfied with a disciplinary decision.

Certain additional details are also required for employees sent to work outside the UK for more than one month.

---

fair. However, we hope you will agree that it is complex and difficult to understand. It could create distrust or even lead to outright dispute in some particular instance. You need to learn how to strike a balance between the simple and the complex.

You might like to know what the consequences of not providing written particulars are likely to be. Bear in mind that Government officials will not arrive to check their existence, and neither you nor your employer are going to be prosecuted for such failures. However, if you fail to provide written particulars within the time limit, an employee can apply to an industrial tribunal, which may then determine particulars of employment as it sees fit.

You may feel this is unlikely to happen. Although it is clearly not good practice to neglect written particulars, so long as relationships with employees remain fair, you could be right. However, redundancies, dismissals or even resignations increase the chances of aggrieved employees making industrial tribunal claims. Complaints that you have failed to provide written particulars will substantially weaken your case at tribunal.

So you would be wise to encourage the managers in your organisation to accept good practice. Indeed, most managers like to be thought of as 'good employers'.

Let's look next at employment protection rights, starting with dismissal.

EMPLOYMENT PROTECTION RIGHTS – DISMISSAL

The right not to be unfairly dismissed

As an employee you will be investing a good proportion of your life in the work of your employer. Most probably you will feel that you make a valuable contribution and represent a good investment, not least because of your ongoing desire to learn and improve your performance. All being well, your employer will be of the same opinion. Unfortunately it is not always the case that employers and employees share the same views. What the employee may see as conscientiousness, the employer may see as being exceedingly pedantic. Single-mindedness may be praised or seen as tunnel vision. The list could continue. So employers and employees do not always measure performance in the same way.

Let's take another example. An employee may need to leave early for a doctor's appointment. If the employee forgets to clock out because of being preoccupied with concern over the appointment, he or she may see this as a simple oversight. The employer may see the same action as an attempt to defraud the company.

These conflicting views highlight a point: it is not acceptable, at least in the case of an employee who has been with the employer for some time, for the employee to be dismissed without some serious attempt to resolve conflict.

These are only two examples. There is a whole range of areas where employers and employees may have different perceptions of each other and of what is expected. Here are a few more:

- the reliability with which the employee attends work

- the quality of the work that is completed

- the language that is used at work

- the achievement of targets

- the attitude to authority

- what constitutes reasonable treatment of the sexes

- what constitutes reasonable treatment of minority groups.

There are other, more serious, areas where behaviour is totally unacceptable (gross misconduct) and where summary dismissal (ie dismissal without notice) may be justified:

- pilfering

- unauthorised absence

- violence

- fraud

- drunkenness.

The danger is that in any of these areas it could be that the employee is falsely accused. (Incidentally, dismissal without notice does not mean 'instant dismissal'. All cases of gross misconduct must be thoroughly investigated before a decision to dismiss is taken.)

Dismissals occur for other reasons too. An employee may become ill and unable to work; a heavy goods vehicle driver could lose his licence; a job may no longer be required; or a reorganisation may lead to fewer jobs even though the same amount of work is being done.

Prior to employment protection legislation, when the decision to dismiss an employee was taken the prime considerations were moral ones. There was no legal obligation to be fair or reasonable. How fair or reasonable dismissal decisions were, in such circumstances, is a matter for conjecture. The consequences for employees then, as now, could be severe. Even though there was low unemployment in the 1950s and 1960s a stigma attached to losing one's job and re-employment could be difficult. At that time the main protection rested in trade union membership, and industrial action in support of dismissed workers did occur. It was not a very satisfactory way to seek redress for unfair dismissals.

Today, employees who have served their employer for a qualifying period have the right not to be unfairly dismissed. The qualifying period has at different times been one year or two years and, as we have already mentioned, may change again. For an employee to be dismissed fairly there must first be a fair reason for the dismissal. Secondly, the employer must act reasonably in arriving at the decision to dismiss.

A fair reason
There are only five potentially fair reasons for dismissal (although the fifth is quite broad):

- *capability* – the inability to perform the type of work for which the employee was employed. This can include health factors.

- *conduct* – failure to meet reasonable expectations. This can include failure to carry out reasonable instructions, bad time-keeping and attendance, as well as gross misconduct, such as theft from the employer.

- *redundancy* – the work for which the employee was employed has ceased or diminished. Here the selection of a particular individual has to be shown to be fair.

- *legal restrictions* – this may apply, for example, when the employee becomes disqualified from driving and the only work available requires the employee to drive.

- *'some other substantial reason'* – this area is established by precedents in case-law. An example might be a reorganisation so long as there is a sound business reason for it. This reason may be used when an employer cannot afford to continue paying on current terms and conditions, dismisses employees for sound business reasons, and offers them a new contract.

Whenever a decision to dismiss is taken it is wise to determine which of the above reasons is the true one. Dismissed employees have the right to ask for written reasons and the reason, or reasons, chosen may need to be defended in a tribunal.

Acting reasonably

Employers may also have to show that they act, or have acted, reasonably and the best way to do this is to follow a fair procedure. In particular the employer has to show that he or she has acted reasonably in reaching the decision to dismiss. Various ACAS publications cover these procedures in detail, and you should consult the advisory handbook on *Discipline at work* in particular (which contains the ACAS Code of Practice). (See the list of reference sources at the end of this chapter.) An historic case, *Polkey* v *A E Dayton Services Ltd* (sometimes referred to simply as *Polkey*), established the necessity always to follow a fair procedure.

Different procedures will be appropriate in different circumstances. Having disciplinary and grievance procedures makes sense for all employers because they provide a framework for resolving conflict fairly. Ill-health issues are more effectively tackled by a specific ill-health procedure. What is a reasonable course of action, when behaviour is within an employee's control, may no longer be reasonable when illness is involved.

Reasonableness is the key to fairness. What may be seen as reasonable procedures for a small employer may be considered to be inadequate procedures for a larger employer. To illustrate this, let's now consider two cases.

After establishing grounds for believing the employee to be guilty, a sole proprietor with 10 employees decides to dismiss an employee for fiddling his bonus. The proprietor may have been the only person to have investigated the allegation, may have been the only person to assess all the evidence, and may have taken the decision to dismiss without consulting anyone else. He might be expected to consider questions such as: Were other employees fiddling their bonus too? Did the employee know, or was it reasonable to expect him to know, that bonus fraud was gross misconduct that could result in dismissal without warning? Although the employer can be expected to have answered such questions, he may nonetheless have to make the final decision without being able to consult anyone else.

In an organisation of 2,000 employees, such a course of action could not rest with one person. More would be expected in terms of the degree of thoroughness. Were the questions posed above properly answered? Was the accusation thoroughly investigated by appropriate people? Was the decision to dismiss taken at a senior level in the organisation? Was an appeal heard in front of people who had not been involved in the original decision?

It is worth noting that fairness will be judged in the light of information available *at the time the decision is made*. An employer must carry out a thorough investigation to gather as much relevant information as is reasonable. He needs to have grounds for his beliefs, eg for believing that an employee is stealing. However, he may make the decision on the balance of probabilities; he does not need proof beyond reasonable doubt. Subsequent, more conclusive, evidence of guilt or innocence is not relevant to the fairness of the decision.

The guidelines contained in the ACAS Code of Practice are very important. The extent to which they are followed, or not followed, will be taken into account when a tribunal judges fairness.

Dismissal

Dismissal takes place when the employer terminates the contract with notice, without notice, or because of actions that effectively breach the contract. Fixed-term contracts that expire without renewal are also dismissals.

There are times when a dismissal is disputed. For example, a supervisor may 'blow up' at an employee, perhaps humiliating the employee in front of his or her colleagues. The employee decides 'enough is enough', goes home, and does not return to work. Has the employee been dismissed or has he or she resigned?

The employer might argue that the supervisor carried out a reprimand, that it was justified, and that it was carried out respectfully – although it may be conceded that colleagues should not have witnessed it. The employer could maintain that the employee has simply resigned. There is therefore no question of dismissal, fair or unfair. Conversely, the ex-employee may produce evidence of previous mistreatment and seek to show that the reprimand was clearly humiliating and very public. He or she might contend that it would be quite intolerable to continue to work in such circumstances. Therefore, because of the actions taken, the employer has dismissed him or her – and unfairly at that.

Were this case to come before an industrial tribunal, the question of dismissal or resignation would be examined very thoroughly. For example, the words used in the reprimand (or emotional outburst), evidence of previous maltreatment, and any protests the employee may have made in the past could all be taken into account. In some cases a tribunal may decide that the employee resigned. In others, it may feel that the employer's treatment of the employee meant trust and confidence had broken down and the employment contract had been broken. This would be 'constructive dismissal', entitling the employee to presume, from the employer's actions, that he or she had been dismissed.

Whether such a dismissal would be unfair might depend on the reason for the reprimand, on whether there had been a thorough investigation, on whether the employee had been formally warned beforehand, and on a range of other factors.

From the employer's viewpoint, sets of circumstances that could lead to an employee claiming constructive dismissal are to be avoided. Once the individual has left the premises, control of the circumstances passes out of the employer's hands. A dismissal may be claimed even if it was not intended. Unless the employee can be tempted back, it becomes too late to ask the employee to explain his or her alleged misconduct. Furthermore, it is too late to carry out an investigation, because the decision has already been taken. The issue has become the employer's misconduct. Once again, the relevant legislation here is the Employment Rights Act 1996.

EMPLOYMENT PROTECTION RIGHTS – DISCRIMINATION

Here we shall be looking at a wide range of areas of potential discrimination; first we examine some broad principles.

Although it may be argued that it makes sound business sense to recruit people solely on their ability to do the job, that judgement is easily influenced by beliefs that are not, in truth, relevant. Even those committed to recruiting on ability can find themselves victims to prejudice that they did not realise they had. More disturbingly, there are still managers who will admit, privately, to unlawful discrimination. For example, they may have prejudices about what constitutes 'men's work' or feel unable to relate to people of a different culture from their own. Unfortunately, in bringing such prejudices to the workplace, they mistakenly believe they serve themselves and their employer better because of it.

As a personnel practitioner you may need to examine your beliefs carefully. It is helpful to read relevant articles in the IPD's magazine, *People Management*, which show how personnel practitioners are positively tackling equal opportunities issues. You could also, valuably, look at the principles of 'Opportunity 2000', which addresses equal opportunities in the public sector. Make sure you know your own organisation's policy and its true attitudes towards women, ethnic minorities, and other groups. These policies should be designed to encourage equal opportunities by educating employees and decision-makers, and by positive actions to address inequality wherever it exists. The spirit or intention of equal opportunities legislation, as well as the letter of the law, is important.

Notwithstanding the merits of your employer's policies, men and women, ethnic minorities, disabled people and many ex-offenders (those who have been sentenced to time in prison) have protection against discrimination. In Northern Ireland it is also illegal to discriminate on religious grounds. So you need to be aware of the legislation.

Keep in mind that applicants as well as employees can be discriminated against. Everyone is eligible for these rights: there are no length of (employment) service requirements. So applicants as well as new employees can take a claim to an industrial tribunal. Furthermore, there are no limits to the amount of compensation that an industrial tribunal can award in cases of discrimination.

Sex discrimination
The social unacceptability of sex discrimination has encouraged appropriate legislation, but much of it has been encouraged in particular by membership of the European Union, in which the Treaty of Rome 1957 provides for equal treatment of men and women.

Discrimination on the grounds of sex or on grounds of people's marital status is unlawful, except in certain special circumstances. However, employers and designated (ie by the Secretary of State) training bodies can take positive action to promote equality. For example, they can set up management courses for women only, if women are underrepresented at managerial levels. Another positive action would be to encourage applications from one sex. But do note that discrimination is not allowed in the actual selection decision.

Both direct and indirect discrimination are illegal. Direct discrimination means allowing gender to influence employment decisions, eg in passing a woman over for promotion in favour of a less-qualified man. Indirect discrimination occurs if conditions that effectively create discrimination are applied. These could be certain criteria on job specifications or advertisements if they tend to preclude women. For example, the Civil

Service used to restrict direct entry to executive grades to those under 26 years old. It can no longer do so, because this would discriminate against women who return to work after bringing up families.

There is a number of *genuine occupational qualifications* (GOQs) that do allow some sex discrimination. Such GOQs cover reasons of privacy, decency, welfare, and authenticity (eg modelling clothes), certain accommodation circumstances, certain single-sex establishments (eg prisons) and, to some extent, work in private homes.

There is an Equal Opportunities Commission (EOC) that works towards eliminating sex discrimination. As part of this work they publish a code of practice to assist employers. If you are to be well informed, you should obtain a copy. Public-sector bodies and progressive employers have responded by preparing equal opportunities policies, as recommended in the code. The legal status of the code may be compared to the highway code. Breaking either code does not constitute an unlawful act in itself, but the codes are to be used as a guide to appropriate driving or behaviour. So failure to follow the EOC code may be taken into account by industrial tribunals in deciding whether to accept claims of discrimination on grounds of sex or marital status.

Maternity rights

Since the 1970s, women have had maternity rights. That is, they have the right not to be unfairly dismissed because of pregnancy, the right to maternity pay, and the right to return to work following maternity leave. Over the years, legislation and case-law have strengthened and enhanced these rights. Dismissal on maternity-related grounds is now automatically unfair, irrespective of length of service or hours of work. All women now have the right to at least 14 weeks' maternity leave and maternity pay. The practical administration of maternity rights and pay is subject to much detail. If you are called on, as well you might be, to administer rights and pay then there are Government publications and other sources, such as updated reference books, which you can use for guidance.

Equal pay

Men and women are entitled to claim equal treatment in respect of pay and conditions. One of the chief areas where equal pay legislation has been effective is the case of part-time employees (see below).

In practice, operation of equal pay is complicated by measurements. Equal treatment requires determination of like work, of work rated as equivalent, and of work of equal value. Equally, of course, what constitutes equal treatment is not easy to measure. Tribunal cases arising under the Equal Pay Act 1970 have frequently led to appeals, proving very expensive for employers. Therefore, despite the complications, every endeavour should be made to ensure equal treatment of men and women.

The main Acts or Parliament of which you should be aware that relate to sex discrimination are:

- Sex Discrimination Acts 1975 and 1986

- Employment Protection (Consolidation) Act 1978

- Equal Pay Act 1970

- Employment Rights Act 1996

Part-time employees
Until the mid-1990s part-time employees could be the 'poor relations' of full-time employees. Frequently they received lower pay, less sickness benefit, and rarely received pension rights. Now, rulings by the European Court of Justice (ECJ) about what constitutes 'pay' effectively give part-timers the right to equal treatment with full-timers. This means they acquire unfair dismissal and redundancy pay rights after the same periods of service as full-timers. Equal treatment covers a range of pay elements such as pensions, severance pay, and sickness benefits. Failure to recognise the right to equal treatment can give rise, at an industrial tribunal, to claims of discrimination or to claims for equal pay.

Racial equality
Some organisations in the retail sector provide good examples of best practice in equal opportunities. They recognise that substantial sectors of the community are of minority ethnic origin. They also recognise that disabled people want to shop for their own goods, and that old as well as young people make good employees. You can see that recognition in the range of goods offered on supermarket shelves, catering for cultural diversity, and in the maturity of staff in certain stores.

Cultural diversity has often developed more slowly in other sectors. Downsizing industrial operations has sometimes limited the opportunities to recruit new employees from other groups. Ethnic minorities tend to be more prevalent in low-pay occupations and in less prosperous industries.

Whether diversity is driven by a desire to be morally right, by commercial pragmatism, or by the law there exists legislation to underpin racial equality in employment and other areas. The legislation is similar to that provided to eliminate sex discrimination. Direct and indirect race discrimination are both outlawed, as is the victimisation of an individual who brings a complaint. There are legislative exceptions for genuine occupational qualifications, but in this case only reasons of authenticity and welfare qualify as genuine occupational qualifications. Positive action, such as the provision of training, to redress an imbalance of particular racial groups is permitted. There is also a Commission for Racial Equality (CRE) which has provided a code of practice; this encourages *ethnic monitoring* to help identify and eliminate race discrimination. You should obtain a copy of the code. The relevant legislation this area is the Race Relations Act 1976.

Disabled people
It may be difficult to come to terms with the fact that a disability has no practical implications for job performance, and yet in many circumstances that is precisely the case. We have to be very wary of 'mind-sets' that lead us to make unjustified assumptions about others.

In Britain comprehensive anti-discrimination legislation now protects disabled people. It is unlawful to treat a disabled person less favourably because he or she is disabled, unless there are very good and relevant reasons in a particular case. Employers are also required to make reasonable adjustments to premises so that disabled applicants or employees are not put at any substantial disadvantage.

There is a code of practice and, again, you should obtain a copy of the code. The relevant legislation is the Disability Discrimination Act 1995.

(For readers' information, the Act was passed in 1995 but its main provisions did not come into force until 2 December 1996.)

Employing ex-offenders

Unless people who have served prison terms can be rehabilitated into employment, it logically follows that they are likely to resort to crime again. So there is some legal protection for those who have received sentences of not more than 30 months. They have the chance to 'wipe the slate clean' after a certain time. The time required varies according to the original sentence. 'Spent' convictions do not have to be disclosed and, even if disclosed, cannot be taken into account in employment decisions. There are, however, exemptions where the work involves access to vulnerable groups such as young people or those with handicaps. The relevant legislation is the Rehabilitation of Offenders Act 1974.

First we take a brief glance at Northern Ireland, where legislation outlaws religious discrimination; then we look at the philosophy behind health and safety, and at legislation introduced over the past few decades.

Religious discrimination – Northern Ireland

Fair employment legislation is further-reaching than any other anti-discrimination law. It demands affirmative action by employers, who have to demonstrate this by strict monitoring of their workforce. Several aspects of the legislation are backed by criminal law. The Fair Employment Commission publishes a code of practice that, if your responsibilities cover Northern Ireland employees, you should obtain.

The relevant legislation is the Fair Employment (Northern Ireland) Act 1989.

Health and Safety

At the IPD Harrogate Conference in 1995, a speaker, Henry Olejnik of Motorola, told how his father lost two fingers in an employment accident in the 1950s. He related how, at that time, such an incident was almost regarded as acceptable. It was seen as 'just the way things are'. The point he went on to make is that we tend to accept the psychological damage (ie stress) that we do to people today as 'just one of those things'. He questioned what judgement future personnel practitioners might make of our current attitudes.

The principal issues here are that, first, we no longer find it acceptable that employees should receive physical injuries at work; secondly, we still tend to accept emotional and psychological injuries as not being the direct responsibility of the employer. But there is continuous progress in attitudes because a mature society, and a caring employer, will look after its people with great care physically and emotionally. In Britain we have seen an increasing legal underpinning of physical and emotional welfare since the early 1960s.

Legislation at that time related chiefly to premises and concerned working conditions, toilets, first-aid boxes, record-keeping, fire precautions, the need for fire escapes, and training for employees so they knew what to do if there was a fire. These provisions are now contained within more recent statutes.

Health and safety legislation introduced in the 1970s

The main relevant Acts were related to factories and then to 'offices, shops and railway premises'. Hazards, though, are different in different industries. In 1974 legislation required employers to produce health and safety policies for their organisations. Because hazards vary from organisation to organisation, the policy is expected to reflect the circumstances of each. This provision is contained in the HASWA, which requires employers to safeguard the health and safety of employees 'as far as reasonably practical'. It covers *all* employees, as well as members of the public who may be exposed to hazards from the employer.

Health and safety policies are a statutory requirement for all employers with five or more employees. A central part of the policy is the general statement. This needs to identify responsibilities for health and safety both at different levels and for specific matters. It has to explain how employees are involved and their acceptance gained. The main policy requirements are summarised in the box below.

Health and safety policies should:

- reflect the plant, equipment, and substances used in the organisation

- address particular hazards

- indicate arrangements for emergencies

- clarify how safety is communicated to employees and visitors on site

- indicate training, safety provision for new employees, etc

- register the regular checks and inspections that are needed.

As well as the requirement for a written health and safety policy, HASWA made managers personally responsible for safety. It also placed a legal obligation on employees to comply with their employer's safety policies. Trade unions were given the right to appoint safety representatives and employers obliged to consult them. Factory inspectors were given powers of enforcement enabling them to issue improvement and prohibition notices. An improvement notice means that a safety aspect has to be improved within a set time. A typical improvement notice might be to reduce the level of dust in the working atmosphere. Prohibition notices mean that equipment or premises cannot be used until changes have been made. A typical prohibition notice may prohibit use of a cutting machine until a guard has been placed on it.

Health and safety at work is overseen by the Health and Safety Commission (HSC), which reports to the Secretary of State and has wide powers to enforce health and safety. It issues a code of practice which, again, you should obtain. The Health and Safety Executive (HSE) enforces the law where responsibilities are not covered by other bodies such as local authorities. All enforcing bodies can appoint inspectors. As well as being able to issue improvement and prohibition notices, inspectors can enter premises without notice and can prosecute employers *and* employees. The relevant legislation is the Health and Safety at Work Act 1974.

Health and safety legislation introduced in the 1980s and 1990s.

To improve enforcement, new reporting requirements were introduced in 1985. These required employers to report 'injuries, diseases and dangerous occurrences' to the HSE or, where appropriate, to the local authority. They also required the keeping of records and an accident book. Factories and all employers with 10 or more people must ensure that all accidents, however minor, are recorded in an accident book.

It had been known for many years that substances encountered at work (eg coal dust and asbestos) caused illness. Research has continually been adding other substances known to cause cancer. So, in 1988 and again in 1994 new Acts required employers to assess health risks that arise from hazardous substances in their work activities. Employers must provide controls that will be effective in protecting employees and anyone else who may be affected by such work. The main obligations on employers are shown in the box below. The relevant legislation is the Reporting of Injuries, Diseases and Dangerous Occurrences Regulations 1995 (RIDDOR) and the Control of Substances Hazardous to Health Regulations 1994 (COSHH).

Controlling substances hazardous to health

The main obligations on employers are to:

- assess the risks and the measures necessary for control of exposure

- prevent or adequately control exposure to hazardous substances

- ensure control methods are used and maintained in efficient working order

- monitor the work environment

- carry out health surveillance on employees where appropriate

- provide information, instruction, and training on risks and precautions.

The European Community is now a major force in British health and safety legislation. Such issues are decided by majority voting in which no nation can exercise a veto. Member nations are obliged to bring domestic legislation into line. The result is a strengthening of existing legislation. The main features of health and safety at work regulations are summarised in the box on page 39.

Health and safety should be managed like other functions, with clear reporting relationships, planning, control, and monitoring. Employees need comprehensive and relevant information and proper training. The regulations require an assessment of the risks to health and safety that arise from the employer's activities. This is to guide the employer as to measures that may need to be taken to comply with statutory requirements. Anyone employing five or more employees is required to record the findings of the assessment.

New minimum standards for the workplace have been set covering such issues as maintenance of equipment, ventilation, temperature, cleanliness, traffic routes, the potential for falling objects, washing, and changing and rest facilities.

Health and safety at work regulations

The following areas require attention by the employer:

- managing health and safety (eg assessing risks)

- workplace health safety and welfare (eg working environment, housekeeping)

- provision and use of work equipment (eg tools to be suitable for their purpose)

- manual handling (eg avoid and assess needs and methods)

- protective equipment (eg ensuring it is properly used)

- display screen equipment (eg satisfying certain minimum requirements).

Work equipment needs to be suitable, properly maintained, and its operatives trained. Controls for starting and stopping machinery have minimum requirements, as do isolation procedures to prevent, for example, equipment starting up while maintenance is being undertaken.

More than a quarter of reported accidents are associated with manual handling, so regulations provide for a particular procedure to assess such risks. There is an obligation to avoid activities where there is a risk of injury, perhaps by automation or mechanisation. Where avoidance is not completely achieved, measures have to be implemented to minimise risks so far as is reasonably practical.

Personal protective equipment should be seen as a last resort after all other methods of improving safety have been considered. Regulations cover its quality, suitability, use, and the requirement for proper training.

Display screen equipment stipulations cover not only computer screens but other forms of display, such as microfiche readers. A variety of risks needs to be assessed, including positioning, posture, and the work environment. Those who use such equipment are entitled to free eye tests and to basic costs of glasses to correct vision defects associated with using the equipment.

Extensive guidance and codes of practice are contained in a series of brochures issued by the HSE, known as the 'six-pack'. They are important to obtain if you have responsibilities in the areas covered. The relevant legislation is the Management of Health and Safety at Work Regulations 1992; the Health and Safety (Display Screen Equipment) Regulations 1992; the Manual Handling Operations Regulations 1992; and the Management of Health and Safety at Work (Amendment) Regulations 1994.

TRADE UNIONS

What is a trade union?
A trade union is an association of members; in which respect it is different from, say, a private company, which has a distinct legal identity. To be a trade union an organisation has to be recognised by a Certification Officer (appointed by the Government) and will usually be a member of the Trades Union Congress (TUC).

Each trade union has its own rules for membership and its own administration and operation. However, there are significant restrictions on union activities brought in by comparatively recent legislation, much of it aimed at 'increasing democracy' within trade unions. For example, at one time, trade unions were able to form 'closed shops' in which only members of particular unions were able to work in particular jobs or companies. This could make it difficult for employees to move jobs unless they carried the right union 'card'. Legislation now outlaws discrimination in employment on the basis of membership or non-membership of a trade union, which effectively prevents closed shops.

Not all employers, of course, welcome unions, and others pride themselves in having such good communications with employees that unionisation has not been desired by those employees. But those employers who recognise a trade union give that union the right to make *collective agreements* with them on behalf of its members.

Shop stewards and collective agreements

Where a union has the majority of a particular group of employees, employers often draw up agreements with a union branch to cover the regulation of shop stewards and the manner in which they conduct their affairs. In return employers will 'recognise' the right of the trade union and its shop stewards to represent its members in relation to their affairs with the employer. Shop stewards are employees who are also representatives of the trade union at the place of work. Where recognised by the employer, they have legal rights to go about a variety of duties related to their trade union responsibilities.

A key part in trade union philosophy, enshrined in the word 'union', is that by joining together employees can counter employers' powers to 'exploit' them. Traditionally it was manual workers that most strongly felt this need, but in recent decades white-collar workers have increasingly become unionised in order to negotiate collectively. The process of negotiating is usually referred to as collective bargaining, and the outcomes of such bargaining as collective agreements.

In order for a trade union to form and negotiate a collective agreement it needs to be able to organise. Thus large groups of employees must feel sufficient mutual interest for them to wish to negotiate together; normally they would join a large and appropriate existing trade union. 'Organisation' also implies the ability of these employees to meet in one place and formulate some common objectives. This has always been easier in large employers such as British Steel or British Aerospace. Industries in which employees are more scattered (such as retail, hotels, and farming) find organisation less practical, and they tend to be less unionised and therefore less likely to have collective agreements.

Collective agreements can cover almost any part of the employer–employee relationship. They may be divided up into substantive and procedural.

Substantive agreements relate to aspects of the contract between employer and employee: for example, the terms and conditions of employment, the rate of pay, or the hours of work. They are often subject to annual negotiation – the annual pay round.

Procedural agreements cover the procedures for regulating the relationship. These provide a means of dealing with issues and resolving conflict in fair and consistent ways. Making procedures part of collective agreements effectively means that, so long as the procedure is followed, unions and management will be in agreement on issues or have clear steps to follow in resolving them. An overall procedural agreement is usually made in order to define the areas in which trade union representation is acknowledged. Areas covered by procedures may include:

- how trade union representatives are appointed

- disputes, and the arbitration procedure if not resolved

- discipline and grievance-handling

- redundancy.

Procedures also enable the organisation to indicate the flexibility that it will allow individual managers in order to ensure that they do not make decisions that counter organisational objectives.

Procedures usually provide for matters to rise through levels of management if they cannot be resolved at a lower level. Generally, they would require matters to be raised at the lowest appropriate level first and then at other levels later. So, for example, under a disciplinary procedure a supervisor may be empowered to warn an employee about his or her behaviour, but not to dismiss. Where such action is necessary, the supervisor will raise the matter to the next level.

Employers often see the principle of collective agreements as beneficial to them. Without such agreements there would be a need to agree terms and conditions with every single employee on an individual basis. It may be necessary, for example, to come to an agreement with workers at a factory which is closing. Where employees are unionised, employers can usually negotiate with a few representative individuals and form an agreement that covers all, or at least a whole category of, employees. In our example it could cover all the workers at the factory. Those covered by collective agreements will have many, if not most, of their employment terms determined by such agreements. Where these terms are not to their liking, then their first port of call is their trade union shop steward – a practice which, in effect, filters out many minor issues.

Despite the advantages that collective agreements can offer, the consequences of industrial action lead the public, who are often inconvenienced by such action, to question collective bargaining. It is to such action that we now turn.

Industrial action
It can be argued that power requires the ability to hurt the other party (and the willingness to do so), even though exercising such power may involve a price to both parties. The desire to avoid that price means that much can be achieved by the knowledge that such power exists and the fact that it is in the interests of both parties to avoid the costs of a breakdown. Don't be deceived by media treatment that likes to emphasise the conflict between 'trade unions and management' just because it is more newsworthy; more often than not, the two parties work together very positively. Nevertheless, the fact that employees may decide to take

industrial action is a source of power in coming to collective agreements. The power balance, of course, shifts continuously with many factors, such as the changing legal background, the level of unemployment, and the market position of an individual employer.

Where employers and employees (represented, usually, by a union) cannot negotiate satisfactory agreements either party may resort to industrial action. At the extreme, employers may use the 'lock-out' option (literally locking employees out of the workplace) or employees may strike. There are other options available, too. Employers may bring in a new contract and dismiss those who do not accept it. (Such dismissals may, or may not, be fair.) Employees may withdraw their goodwill and take all kinds of actions, of which 'working to rule' (interpreting rules so precisely that little practical work is accomplished) and overtime bans are typical. Significantly, it is possible for skilful manipulation to distort the picture of who is responsible for the breakdown of talks.

It therefore follows that great skill and care is required and that sensitive industrial relations issues will be probably handled by the most senior and the most experienced people in your organisation. You should be aware, too, that complex legislation regulates industrial action, that there is a need for a union to hold secret ballots, and that employees can exercise a right not to strike.

If circumstances mean that you cannot avoid involvement in a dispute, always seek appropriate advice. In a large organisation this will be from more senior members of the personnel department. In a small organisation ACAS is likely to be your most important source.

ACAS is a body set up by the Government but which is required to act impartially in seeking to promote good industrial relations. Its services are available both to employers and individuals, and it receives enquiries from both sources in comparable proportions. It can be called in by parties that are failing to agree on employment matters and it will endeavour to conciliate (essentially getting the parties to talk their problems through), appoint mediators (to suggest solutions to the parties), or appoint an arbitrator, who must have the full consent of both parties. In this latter case the parties agree in advance to accept the arbitrator's decision. The result is that ACAS officials have a huge bank of experience in industrial conflict and are therefore excellently placed to assist in industrial relations.

The relevant legislation is the Trade Union and Labour Relations (Consolidation) Act 1992.

THE ROLE OF PERSONNEL PRACTITIONERS

In employing you in the personnel function, your organisation will be looking to you and your colleagues to help keep its activities in line with legislative requirements, if not to go further and help it to adopt best practices. But don't be surprised if, from time to time, colleagues outside the function do not seem as committed to such premises as you might expect. Let's have a look at your likely roles.

An advisory role to line managers
To be effective you need to know and understand the basics of employment law and to know where to go to find more detailed information in specific

instances. This chapter has outlined the main aspects of employment law but it can only provide general guidance. Minor details of law can become very important in specific instances, so always check the detail if you have decisions to make. Furthermore, the legal situation changes continually both in response to legislation and in the way in which it is interpreted. To help you, there is a wide range of reference books available; those that are regularly updated are particularly valuable. It is important that you do not exceed your understanding of the law, so, if you are in any doubt, always seek further advice. This would normally be from senior colleagues or from bodies such as ACAS. They have offices in all regions of the United Kingdom except Northern Ireland, where similar services are available from the Labour Relations Agency.

A decision-making role

From time to time you may be called on to make decisions that require an understanding of employment law. As an example, you might be involved in the decision to move employees from one place of work to another. While you must act within a legally defensible position, be wary of invoking the law with employees in a direct fashion. It would be inappropriate, for example, simply to demand that an employee moved his place of work just because, five years ago, he signed a contract which included such a clause. However, much can be achieved by consultation and negotiation. Remember that you are expected to act fairly and reasonably and, in this context, that would mean consulting with the employee about the issue. So, acting fairly and reasonably is not just a moral requirement but a legal necessity. Therefore, as a personnel practitioner, you may often find the law supporting you in your desire to 'do the right thing'.

An overseeing role

If you maintain regular contact with your colleagues by 'walking the floor' in workshops and offices or through other network activities, then you will often become aware of potential legal problems or potential disputes that can be 'nipped in the bud'. Some overseeing roles may need to be more formalised, such as equal opportunities monitoring. Health and safety audits also need to be formal, although if you have specific responsibilities in this area you should seek further appropriate training.

An administrative role

This may be your key role, ensuring good accessible records of contracts, and keeping equal opportunities records, health and safety records, and disciplinary records. Your diligence in this area may attract scant attention, and even a little resistance. But when problems arise these good records can afford real protection for employers and managers who may need to defend their actions at a tribunal or in other courts.

A training or educational role

If line managers are to take true responsibility for personnel matters – a direction in which many organisations are progressing – then they too will need an understanding of employment law. The very process of passing on your own understanding will force you to become more familiar with the subject and should reinforce your own role as 'the expert' in your organisation.

ACTIVITIES

1 Think about your own organisation. How do managers and employees view the effect of law on employment? Do managers use it to control or manage people? If so, how? Are employees reassured by their employment rights? What do you think of the attitudes in your organisation? Write down your thoughts and discuss them with one of your learning sources, as described in the Introduction to this book.

2 In your capacity as a personnel practitioner, assume you are invited to assist a manager at an interview. You fear that the manager has no intention of accepting a woman for the vacancy, despite two of the five interviewees being women. Write down what you would do. Discuss your intentions with one of your learning sources.

3 Look at your organisation's health and safety policy. Is it readily available? Compare it to the guidelines provided in the relevant section above – does it address each area? Is it up-to-date? Make a list of any matters that you think should be addressed.

4 Pick a topical health and safety issue in your department or organisation: for example, the use of computer screens. Research the appropriate legislation and good practice. Compare the legislation and good practice with what actually happens. Make a note of suitable improvements.

REFERENCES AND FURTHER READING

FOWLER A. (1994) 'How to produce a health and safety policy'. *Personnel Management Plus*. January. pp24–5.

HODGES C. (1994) 'Personal help from personnel'. *Personnel Management Plus*. January. pp22–3.

LEWIS D. (1997) *Essentials of employment law*. 5th ed. London, Institute of Personnel and Development.

PICKARD J. (1996) 'The legal fight for work place justice'. *People Management*. 29 August. pp32–5.

Polkey v *A E Dayton Services Ltd*. House of Lords [1987] Industrial Relations Law Reports 503.

TORRINGTON D. *and* HALL L. (1991) *Personnel management*. Hemel Hempstead, Prentice Hall.

See also the IPD's *Law and Employment* series:

AIKIN O. (1997) *Contracts*. 2nd ed. London, Institute of Personnel and Development.

CLARKE L. (1995) *Discrimination*. 2nd ed. London, Institute of Personnel and Development.

EARNSHAW J. *and* COOPER C. (1996) *Stress and employer liability*. London, Institute of Personnel and Development.

FOWLER A. (1993) *Redundancy*. London, Institute of Personnel and Development.

GREENHALGH R. (1995) *Industrial tribunals*. 2nd ed. London, Institute of Personnel and Development.

JAMES P. *and* LEWIS D. (1992) *Discipline*. London, Institute of Personnel and Development.

ADVISORY, CONCILIATION AND ARBITRATION SERVICE. (amended 1989) *Advisory handbook on discipline at work*. Leicester, ACAS. (This includes the *Code of practice on disciplinary practice* and *Procedures in employment*. These and other advisory handbooks and booklets are available from: ACAS Reader Ltd, P.O. Box 16, Earl Shilton, Leicester, LE9 8ZZ; tel. 01455 852 225.)

The following codes of practice are available from HMSO Publications Centre (mail, fax, and telephone orders only), P.O. Box 276, London, SW8 5DT; tel. 0171 873 9090:

Code of practice: equal opportunities policies, procedures and practices in employment. (1985) London, HMSO.

Code of practice: for the elimination of discrimination in the field of employment against disabled persons or persons who have had a disability. (1996) London, HMSO.

Code of practice on equal pay. (1997) London, HMSO.

See also:

Disability Discrimination Act 1995. Industrial Relations Law Bulletin. No. 535, December 1995.

The following is available from the Commission for Racial Equality, Elliot House, 10–12 Allington Street, London, SW1E 5EH; tel. 0171 828 7022:

Code of practice: for the elimination of racial discrimination and the promotion of equality of opportunity in employment. (1984) London, CRE.

See also:

Fair Employment (Northern Ireland) Code of practice. (1989) Belfast, Department of Economic Development. Available from HMSO, 80 Chichester Street, Belfast, BT1 4JY.

The following are available from the Health and Safety Executive, HSE Books, P.O. Box 1999, Sudbury, Suffolk, CO10 6FS (tel. 01787 881 165):

Everyone's guide to RIDDOR 1995 (HSE 31). (1996) London, HSE Books.

Five steps to successful health and safety management: special help for directors and managers (INDG 132). (1992) London, HSE Books.

Getting to grips with manual handling: a short guide for employers (INDG 143). (1995) London, HSE Books.

Health and safety regulations: a short guide (HSE 13). (1995) London, HSE Books.

HSE small firms strategy. (1997) London, HSE Books.

A short guide to the personal protective equipment at work regulations (INDG 174). (1992) London, HSE Books.

Working with VDUs (INDG 6). (1994) London, HSE Books.

Workplace health, safety and welfare: a short guide for managers (INDG 244). (1995) London, HSE Books.

Writing a safety policy statement: advice to employers (HSC 6). (1990) London, HSE Books.

See also IPD *Guides* and *Key facts* on employment issues. These replace the former IPM and ITD codes and statements, and are available from the Communications Department, IPD House, Camp Road, London, SW19 4UX.

There is also a variety of publications of general relevance to employment law and personnel work available from Croner Publications Ltd, Croner House, London Road, Kingston on Thames, Surrey KT2 6SR (tel. 0181 547 3333).

4 Recruitment and selection

INTRODUCTION

In the past, personnel practitioners have spent a great deal of their time engaged in the activities associated with the recruitment and selection of staff. Major recruitment campaigns have been carried out to recruit and select replacement staff, staff with specialist skills, trainees, graduates etc. The personnel practitioner consequently gained a great deal of experience in the administrative and interviewing activities associated with staffing the organisation. In larger organisations specialist recruitment officers were appointed, whose main role was to ensure that (to borrow a time-honoured expression) they employed 'the right people in the right jobs at the right time'. Often the evaluation process stopped at the point of entry to the organisation as everyone just breathed a sigh of relief that, for the time being, the staffing level was correct. We shall see in the concluding stages of this chapter that evaluation should continue for a period of up to 12 months after appointment in order to ensure that the whole process is as cost-effective as possible.

The employment situation has in recent years shifted from a seller's to a buyer's market. In the mid-1990s the economic climate dictated that most organisations did not expand but downsize, so that the emphasis changed from the 'input' side of the staffing process, ie recruitment, to the 'output' side, ie effecting terminations of short-term contracts, redundancies, and early retirements. In any event, the same level of care and attention needs to be paid to the recruitment and selection process in order to ensure that the organisation's human resource (HR) requirements are satisfied in as cost-effective a manner as possible.

Further, whatever the economic climate, the HR planning process is by no means simple. Organisations need to predict their HR requirements (eg numbers, skills, and levels of responsibility) in accordance with future corporate objectives. Even if it is obvious that fewer staff will be required in the future than currently, it is highly unlikely that a recruitment freeze could be effective for an extended period of time if the organisation is to remain viable. There are many factors to be taken into consideration (eg existing skills, training and development provision, career progression and labour turnover), and it would be an unusual – and fortunate – employer that did not need to look at the external labour market to 'buy in' new skills and abilities for key posts.

We shall now explain why the interlinked activities of recruitment and selection are so important, before outlining the relevant legislation and the practical issues involved in the recruitment and selection of staff. We shall be covering the key recruitment stages of job analysis and advertising, and the selection processes of candidate data collection (including interviewing), assessment, and comparison. Finally, the induction and evaluation processes and the various roles played by personnel practitioners will be considered.

WHY ARE RECRUITMENT AND SELECTION IMPORTANT?

We have commented on the fact that the proportion of time spent by personnel practitioners and line managers in recruiting and selecting staff has decreased significantly in recent years in many organisations. Despite the overall decrease in new staff appointments, it is crucial that the selection choices result from a thorough and systematic process. (In order not to be too gloomy, it is worth pointing out that not all organisations are contracting in size, and there are many success stories from which to draw comfort.) As personnel practitioners, you will need to be knowledgeable about the wider issues involving recruitment and selection decisions, such as legislation and good practice, and the range of recruitment sources and selection methods, as well as being skilled in interviewing and assessing potential employees.

Examples of poor practice in recruitment and selection decisions and their possible outcomes are listed below:

- When a job becomes vacant, failure to question whether it ought to be redesigned by making changes to, say, the level of responsibility, remuneration package, hours of work, working methods and reporting lines – or even whether it should be filled at all (ie where the work could be absorbed by existing members of staff) – will have cost implications, because the job has not been designed to suit the current needs and the possibility of potential savings has been ignored.

- A hurried attempt to meet an advertising deadline in the local paper may result in inaccurate copy which, at the very least, misleads potential applicants and, at worst, discourages them from applying.

- Failure to carry out effective research into advertising media for a specialist post resulting in a lower standard of applicants than envisaged, and therefore the necessity to readvertise in, say, a specialist journal will project a poor image of the personnel department or of whoever was responsible.

- Untrained interviewers projecting a poor public relations image of the organisation to prospective employees and the use of inadvisable lines of questioning (eg family circumstances) may lead to claims of sex discrimination.

- Untrained and inexperienced observers used to assess too many candidates against too many criteria in a lengthy group exercise during an assessment centre may lead to invalid results.

- A decision to offer posts to candidates who performed 'best on the day' even though they fell short of the requirements defined as essential for performing the job satisfactorily (see the personnel specification section below) may result in their leaving or being dismissed in the short term or requiring more training than was envisaged in the long term.

We could go on! The important factor to note is that all of the above examples of poor practice result in unnecessary costs to the organisation. Advertising alone is expensive, but once you move beyond a wasted advertising opportunity to the salary costs of an unsuitable employee or the potential cost of a lost industrial tribunal case, then you may be facing the loss of thousands of pounds (and the wrath of higher management).

THE LEGISLATION

Before moving on to look at the mechanisms of recruitment and selection, we are going to consider in outline only the relevant legislation before moving on to consider the important issue of good practice. The legislation is referred to and commented on throughout this chapter as well as being specifically referred to in Chapter 3. You should be aware of the impact of the following pieces of legislation:

- Sex Discrimination Acts 1975 and 1986

- Race Relations Act 1976

- Disability Discrimination Act 1995.

In simple terms, the above Acts make it unlawful for organisations to take into account a person's gender, marital status, colour, race, nationality, ethnic or national origin, or disability in employment decisions. Here we are specifically concerned with decisions at the point of access to the organisation, but training, promotion and termination decisions are also covered.

The enforcement agencies associated with the promotion of equal opportunities in the workplace are the Commission for Racial Equality (CRE) and the Equal Opportunities Commission (EOC) for race and sex discrimination respectively. They have both issued codes of practice giving guidance to employers on how to comply with the legislation (see the legislative acts/codes section at the end of this chapter). For instance, it is recommended that employers have written equal opportunities policies, procedures for making complaints, monitoring arrangements, and that they take positive action steps to redress any imbalances in the make-up (gender or race profile) of their employees by, for example, wider advertising, special needs training, flexible working hours arrangements, and help with childcare.

As for the disability legislation, there is no corresponding enforcement agency. A National Disability Council (NDC) has been set up, but the employment aspects of the legislation will not be covered by the NDC but by the existing National Advisory Council on Employment of People with Disabilities (NACEPD). Both councils, unlike the CRE and EOC, cannot give direct advice and support. A code of practice has been issued with the intention of helping employers to get to grips with this wide-ranging legislation.

So far we have considered only those groups of employees who are covered by legislative provisions. Many leading organisations in the equal opportunities field have policies that include reference to groups not specifically covered by the legislation. This good practice shows that they 'cast the net' wider to ensure that employees or potential employees are also not discriminated against because of their age, religion, sexual orientation etc.

You are strongly advised to read the IPD Guides and Key Facts publications listed at the end of this chapter under References and Further Reading for more guidance on best practice in the fields of recruitment and selection and equal opportunities.

OVERVIEW

Continuing on the theme of good practice, we are now at the stage of considering the practical issues relevant to recruitment and selection. We shall, for simplicity's sake, be considering these two processes separately, but it is obvious they are closely interlinked, as demonstrated by the simple flow chart in Figure 1.

THE RECRUITMENT PROCESS

There are two major stages involved here: job analysis and advertising. We have already looked at examples of the potential pitfalls of inactivity, hurry, or sheer carelessness at these and other stages. Both job analysis and advertising will often fall within your activities as a personnel practitioner, and you should ensure that you take a proactive stance here. With regard to job analysis, however, you should seek to ensure that line managers retain responsibility and ownership for this activity for their own staff, and do not view this purely as a personnel function. Regarding advertising, the design and placing of advertisements is usually handled centrally, ie by personnel practitioners, to maximise control and minimise costs. We will consider the two stages below.

Job analysis
There are three elements in job analysis:

- field study

- job descriptions

- personnel specifications.

We shall take each in turn.

Field study
In order to acquire information about a job and the skills and qualities required of a person suited to that job, we need first to carry out a thorough analysis of the job and its organisational environment. There are various techniques for so doing, and these include observation, questionnaires, interviews, self-reports, work diaries, group discussions, reviewing critical incidents, and check-lists. The aim is to answer the following questions:

- What is the job-holder expected to do?

- How is the job performed?

Figure 1 Recruitment and selection flow chart

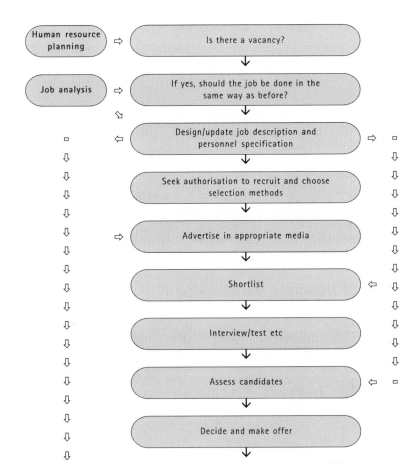

The black arrows indicate the sequence of events, the white arrows where information from one stage is fed into another. For instance, the scrutinising of job applications for shortlisting purposes should not be carried out as a separate event but be based on the information provided by the personnel specification on the characteristics and qualities sought. In fact, application forms, if used, should be so designed that the reader does not have to 'read between the lines' but can easily make a judgement as to whether applicants possess the characteristics or qualities deemed essential.

NB: It is important to examine at each stage areas where discrimination could occur and take preventative action.

- What skills are required and what is the level of those skills?

- Should the job be reorganised (eg change to hours, level of responsibility, duties incorporated into other posts)?

The field study stage should provide information that can then be formulated into 'user-friendly' documents, ie the job description and the personnel specification.

Job description

In simple terms, this describes the job! Organisations usually have their own standardised formats for job descriptions and, though they vary enormously, generally they include the following sections:

- *identification data*: job title, department, pay grade, location

- *organisational data*: responsible to and for, other working relationships

- *job summary*: a brief statement of why the job exists

- *job content*: a breakdown of the key activities in a summarised format (more senior posts may also cover the standards of performance expected)

- *miscellaneous*: covering unusual arrangements such as shift-working, a need to be mobile, casual car user allowance.

Personnel specification

Other commonly used terms are the 'person specification' or 'job specification'. All three are used to describe 'the ideal person for the job'. (We would recommend that you use the term 'personnel specification' or 'person specification' but avoid the term 'job specification' because it is uncomfortably close in sound to the term 'job description', and is therefore easy to confuse in meaning.) Once again, personnel specifications vary in content and format depending on the 'house style'. We see, in examples of personnel specifications, the terms 'skills', 'knowledge', 'qualities' and, more recently, 'competencies' used, but basically their purpose is the same: to set down the minimum requirements that an applicant must possess before being considered for a vacancy. Further, most personnel specifications go beyond stating the minimum (essential) requirements and also state other (desirable) requirements, as demonstrated in Table 3.

Thus a successful candidate will be expected already to possess all the essential requirements and to be capable of, or have the potential to be trained to, an acceptable standard in the desirable ones. You should take note that *all* the requirements must be *realistic* and *justifiable*. An example where this would not be so is as follows:

- A stipulation that candidates for a supervisory position be fluent in Urdu, Bengali, Welsh, and English and be physically strong enough to handle sheets of lead for sustained periods of time would be unrealistic: there are simply not enough people meeting those requirements out there in the labour market (particularly for the salary on offer!).

- The above requirements would also be unjustifiable if in reality the job did not involve communications in all the specified languages or did not entail the need to lift heavy items for sustained periods. (It would also undoubtedly be safer to provide special lifting equipment.)

Table 3 Example personnel specification form

	Company Name		
Job title:	Personnel Manager		
Department:	Personnel		
	Essential requirement	Desirable requirement	Method of assessment
Qualifications	Graduate calibre (ie at least two good A levels). IPD qualified.	Graduate in relevant subject. MIPD.	Application form and certificate check.
Experience	Minimum of three years' experience in generalist personnel work at personnel officer level.	Five or more years' relevant experience in a unionised environment.	Application form, interview, and references.
Knowledge and Skills	Up-to-date knowledge of employment legislation. Organisational skills. Financial awareness. Computer literate.	Knowledge and skills in employee relations and negotiating. Experience of working with XYZ personnel information system.	Application form, interview, and role-play plus references.
Personal Qualities	Good communicator – written and oral skills, good judgement, confident, persuasive, approachable, dependable, uses initiative, average numeracy.		Application form, interview, group exercises, tests, and references.
Motivation and Expectations	Desire to develop personnel function. High expectations of self and others.		Application form, interview, and references.
Overall Appearance	Well presented. Clear speech.		Interview.

In any event, care must be taken to ensure that personnel specification requirements do not discriminate either directly or indirectly on the grounds of race, sex, or disability.

Assuming that we have decided there is a vacancy to be filled, that we have carried out our job analysis and designed our working documents (the job description and the personnel specification), and that we have permission to do so, we are now ready to advertise.

Advertising

Advertising can be a very expensive activity, especially if we get it wrong. It can be tempting to sit back and congratulate ourselves on a thorough job analysis which resulted in workable and user-friendly documents, ie the job description and the personnel specification. We need, however, to be just as systematic and methodical in our approach to advertising the vacancy in terms of the content and design, the timing of the advertisement, and our choice of media.

In commencing the advertising process you need first to be aware of the sources of possible recruits:

- existing employees, ie internal recruitment
- jobcentres
- employment agencies or recruitment consultants
- advertising
  - shop windows or factory gates
  - local and national newspapers
  - the ethnic press, publications, and meeting venues
  - professional, specialist, or technical journals
  - local radio
  - television
  - the Internet
- the 'Milk Round'
- word of mouth (personal recommendations)
- networking
- headhunters
- 'waiting lists' or speculative queries
- open days
- liaison with schools and colleges.

Different sources are appropriate depending on the group of potential applicants that you wish to target. For instance, you may decide to use the free facilities of the jobcentre for semi-skilled positions, especially when you expect to find a wealth of unemployed talent in the immediate locality. However, if you wish to attract specialist or technical personnel you will probably need to spread the net further and make use of national newspapers and appropriate journals. This will obviously be more expensive, but there is also a cost attached to not filling a key post, eg in overtime payments and missed opportunities. We can assert that an advertisement is cost-effective only when it is concisely worded, well designed, and attracts a sufficient number of suitably qualified candidates.

You should note that in order to comply with equal opportunities legislation vacancies should be advertised as widely as possible. Relying entirely on internal recruitment, 'on file' applications, or personal recommendations may leave the organisation open to criticism, and is highly unlikely to move it towards an appropriate gender or race balance in its staff profile.

The *timing* of the advertisement is also of crucial importance, especially when advertising in newspapers and journals. You must ensure that:

- for the local press, you choose the day job-seekers know that jobs will appear

- you avoid advertising just before a holiday or shutdown period, because you may miss potential applicants who are on holiday or disillusion others who cannot contact the organisation for further information

- you check the dates for final copy and meet them in order to avoid unnecessary delays in recruitment (this can be protracted if using monthly publications).

Another important tip is that you need to be very specific regarding the section of the publication in which you wish to place your advertisement. Odd-numbered pages are generally more widely read than even-numbered ones, but also you do not want your advertisement for a new chief executive to be lost among the double-glazing sales pitches or the lonely hearts column!

We shall now concentrate on the *design* and *content* of the advertisements themselves. One of the most popular mnemonics used by personnel practitioners is AIDA. This provides a guide to successful advertising by highlighting the four steps below:

*A*ttention

*I*nterest

*D*esire

*A*ction

To work, an advertisement must catch the *attention* of the target audience and hold the reader's *interest* so that the whole message is read. Further, it should arouse *desire* for the opportunity offered and stimulate *action* in the form of applications from the target audience.

This may be easier said than done, but studying examples of advertisements is very useful for highlighting good and bad practices. An example of an advertisement that fails to comply with AIDA is provided below; it was found in the General Appointments section of the *Daily Telegraph* on a Monday, and is reproduced below without reference to the real organisation in order to avoid embarrassment.

FINANCIAL CONTROLLER

This is an exciting opportunity to join one of England's top Football Clubs. The successful candidate will be a qualified, experienced accountant used to working in a commercial environment who understands the importance of 'bottom line' and has a flair for evaluating systems and ideas for their business potential and cost effectiveness.

Reporting to the Company Secretary, you will be responsible for the financial control of all Club operations.

Age is not important, a dynamic, enthusiastic attitude is. A competitive salary will be offered together with a full executive benefits package. Please send your CV to:

G Taylor, Neversaydie Football Club, Green Lane, Neverton.

As you can see, the advertisement is poorly located (how many potential financial controllers will be reading this section of the *Daily Telegraph* on a Monday?), is not designed to grab your *attention* or hold your *interest* (the fact that the job would entail working for a football club is not capitalised upon at all), gives vague and limited information about the job and the person sought and so fails to arouse *desire* (further, there is no indication of the salary banding), and it is unclear about the application procedure ie the *action* that should follow, because there is no contact number for further information and no closing date. (See the Activities section at the end of this chapter for further reference to this example.)

So what should we do to avoid making mistakes in advertising? There are no golden rules, but generally an advertisement, drawing on and summarising the job description and the personnel specification, should be composed as follows:

- job title/location/salary (these are of key interest to job-seekers)

- brief description of the job

- brief description of the nature of the organisation (unless very well known)

- brief description of the 'ideal person' (highlighting, as a minimum, the essential requirements)

- organisational benefits and facilities (if attractive)

- unique features (such as hours of work, need for mobility, accommodation provision)

- application procedure and closing date

- reference number (if used)

- equal opportunities statement.

In essence, you must give enough information about the job – to target the right people – and the person required – to attract suitable candidates only to apply. The *image* portrayed should be inviting but also reflective of the style and culture of the organisation. For instance, an eye-catching headline seeking an 'Action Man or Wonder Woman' would probably not be appropriate for a filing clerk's post in a local authority, but has been successfully used for a security officer's role in a large toy store.

Assuming that your advertisement has attracted a manageable number of suitably qualified and experienced candidates, we shall now move on to the important stage of selecting the right candidate. Please note that, as we indicated earlier, the processes of recruitment and selection are not discrete, so in fact you should by now have made the decision on which selection methods you wish to use (see Figure 1, page 51).

THE SELECTION PROCESS

You should make your decision on the successful candidate as a result of

- candidate data collection

- candidate assessment

• comparison.

You should always avoid making a simple comparison of candidates with each other as this is likely to be highly subjective and will lead to an offer of the position to the candidate who was deemed to be 'the best on the day'. Instead you should use the personnel specification and, at each stage, compare the candidates with the essential and desirable requirements listed.

Candidate data collection
Information is gathered about candidates through:

• application forms

• curricula vitae (CVs)

• interview performances

• tests (ranging from physical, intelligence, and aptitude through to personality)

• appraisals (for internal candidates)

• references

• assessment centre performances (generally used only for large-scale recruitment and more senior positions).

In order for this process to be directed at achieving your aim, ie to recruit the person who most closely fits your personnel specification profile, you should ensure that you collect only relevant information about the candidates. For example, an applicant's bizarre taste in music or socks is unlikely to be relevant and can lead, like discussions of which football team he or she supports, to unfounded prejudices. We are now going to consider one of the above methods, the interview, in more detail. It is not our intention to consider the use of tests and assessment centres in any more detail, but suffice it to say that they are increasing in popularity and are designed to provide more information about the candidate than can be gained by exclusive use of the much-maligned interview. Tests and assessment centres have also usually been validated to see whether the tests and exercises in them adequately measure relevant characteristics and abilities in order to predict job success. There is a wealth of reading and commentary on this area for your further enlightenment. Articles in the IPD's *People Management* magazine would be a useful starting-place; see also the IPD publications listed under References and Further Reading at the end of this chapter.

The interview
Unlike tests and assessment centres, the interview, as a selection tool, has been much criticised for its lack of validity (the results of interviewing have been found to be only slightly higher than random selection at predicting future success in the job!). Nevertheless, any coverage of recruitment and selection would be incomplete without reference to 'the interview'. Though we can see the pitfalls of its use, few appointments are made without the interview playing some role. You should note that the effectiveness of interviews can be improved by thorough preparation and by ensuring that all the questions asked are relevant (and seen to be relevant) to the job.

The majority of employing organisations still use interviews as a crucial stage before deciding on new appointments because they see that interviews can be useful for:

- verifying information

- exploring omissions

- checking assumptions

- providing information to the candidate.

In fact, candidates themselves seem equally loath to dispense entirely with interviews. Many feel that the interview provides the only opportunity for them to reveal their personalities and to 'sell' themselves to the employer. In recent times there has been a move towards more structured, job-specific interviews which place less emphasis on establishing rapport and 'getting to know' the candidate. This highly focused approach entails the need to answer a specified number of questions designed to show whether the candidate has the relevant experience and qualities or not. A 'victim' of this approach was heard to complain that 'They might as well have interviewed me over the telephone, as they didn't find out anything about me at all.' The logic of this trend is obvious and commendable, but perhaps a balance of the job-specific and more 'human' approaches would be advisable.

Regarding the practical aspects of the interviewing process, you need to consider the structure of the interview and the skills involved. Provided below are, first, another mnemonic to remind you of a recommended structure for the interview process and, secondly, a check-list for successful interviewing which identifies the necessary skills.

The structure of the interview should, in simple terms, follow the mnemonic WASP:

*W*elcome

*A*cquire – What information do you have?

        – What else do you need?

        – What should you check?

*S*upply – What information should you impart?

*P*art

Thus you should bear WASP in mind when drawing up your list of questions for interviewees. If you are involved in a panel interview, each member of the panel can lead a different section of questions while still maintaining a logical structure overall. A check-list for successful interviewing practice and an examination of the types of questions to be used and avoided are reproduced in Tables 4 and 5. Note, however, that the check-list in Table 4 is likely, with some adaptation, to be applicable to a large number of interviewing situations, not just those designed for staff selection purposes.

Table 4 Interviewing check-list

BEFORE

- Familiarise yourself with the job description and personnel specification.
- Read the application form and CV.
- Meet the rest of the interview panel to agree the list of questions and roles to be played eg chair, scribe, timekeeper.
- Arrange the interview at an appropriate time and place.
- Book the venue.
- Inform the applicant well in advance, providing details of location, time, expected duration, need for preparation, travel expense provisions, number of stages in the selection process etc.
- Confirm the arrangements with the panel members.
- Notify Security and Reception of the arrangements.
- Ensure that the venue is private and that interruptions will not occur.
- Allow enough time between interviews for breaks, discussions, and completion of assessment forms and, at the end of all the interviews, for a full review.

DURING

- Start on time.
- Start with a welcome.
- Seek to establish rapport.
- Explain the purpose of the interview and the stage in the selection process.
- Ask relevant questions (see Table 5).
- Allow the applicant to do the majority of the talking.
- Listen actively.
- Do not seek to fill silences (or you may discourage the candidate from providing more information).
- Observe non-oral behaviour (and check anomalies between this and the oral messages).
- Check gaps, omissions, or contradictions.
- Check claims *re* level and type of experience.
- Use a logical sequence of questions and provide links between sections.
- Provide brief information on the job and organisation.
- Allow sufficient time for the applicant's questions.
- Take brief notes.
- Keep control of the content and timing.
- Summarise.
- Close on a positive note – thank the candidate and reiterate the next stage of the process.

AFTERWARDS

- Compare the information gained about the applicant with the personnel specification requirements.
- Complete the assessment form and keep proper records.
- Follow up the interview with the appropriate documentation eg invitation to the next stage, rejection letter.

Table 5 **Types of interview questions**

Generally questions should be:

open   to encourage full reponses
eg 'Tell me about...'

probing to check information provided in the application or interview
eg What, Why, How, Explain...

Probing questions include hypothetical or situational questions to elicit practical experience or judgement; and 'contrary evidence' questions to check an assumption made about the candidate by seeking evidence to the contrary.

Closed questions, ie those demanding a yes or no response, should be used only for clarification or control eg bringing a line of questioning to its conclusion.

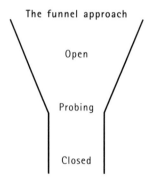

The funnel approach

Open

Probing

Closed

We recommend a *funnelling* approach, as indicated above. You should start with an *open* question, eg 'Tell me about your current responsibilities', followed by progressively narrower *probing* questions, eg 'What experience have you had of formal negotiating situations?' At the end of this section of questioning you should use a *closed* question such as 'So would it be accurate to say that you have had limited experience in formal negotiating situations, and if you are successful in being offered this vacancy, you would welcome specialist training in this area?' The candidate is very likely to say yes, effectively bringing about a 'full stop' to this section. You should then provide a link to the next section of questioning eg 'Thank you for your responses to those questions; we will now move on to discuss...'.

The following types of questions should generally be avoided:

leading eg 'You are fully trained in the use of an XYZ Personnel Information
System, aren't you?'
(The candidate knows exactly what answer you are looking for here!)

multiple eg 'Tell us about your educational background, your career history to
date, and your strengths and weaknesses.'
(By the time the candidate has finished telling you about his or her educational qualifications, you will probably both have forgotten what else you asked. Further, a clever candidate will undoubtedly tell you about his or her strengths but ignore the issue of weaknesses!)

If you do fall into either of the above traps, it is relatively easy to rectify your mistake by asking additional probing questions. Keeping brief notes, both of the candidate's responses and the further questions that you feel it necessary to ask, will help you here.

We have seen that we need to gather a range of data about our candidates via various methods such as the application form and the interview. We shall now consider candidate assessment.

Candidate assessment

In assessing our candidates, we need to evaluate each candidate against the job-relevant criteria detailed in the personnel specification and reach a considered and objective judgement in each case. Here your skills in defining those criteria in very specific and measurable terms should stand you in good stead. Using the example personnel specification form shown in Table 3 (see page 53), we can see that all the requirements should really be defined further. For example, 'good oral communicator' means different things to different people. We need to specify whether our successful candidate should be an articulate, experienced, and polished presenter or simply have a reasonably good vocabulary.

At the short-listing stage you are likely to have only the information contained on the application form. If this has been well designed it should be relatively easy to filter out those candidates who do not meet the minimum (essential) requirements. (Curricula vitae (CVs) are often used at this initial short-listing stage, but because they are not standardised and often contain incomplete information, they may be much less useful here.) If you still have a large number of potentially suitable candidates, you may short-list further by producing a list of candidates who appear to possess a number of the desirable requirements also. Interviews, tests, and exercises can then be used to gain more information on your short-listed candidates. Depending on the number of suitable applicants and the seniority of the post, the selection process may consist of one, two, or even three stages (with a different combination of selection methods and personnel involvement at each stage).

Comparison

Here you are comparing the candidate assessment with the personnel specification and looking for the 'closest fit'. The candidate who most closely matches the 'ideal person' described in your personnel specification should be offered the vacancy. You do not select the person who performs 'best' overall, because this is likely to result in an overqualified person (ie in excess of your requirements) or an underqualified person (ie all the candidates fell short of your requirements) being recruited. If you are confident that you have carried out a systematic job analysis, you should realise that those candidates who appear to be overqualified for your needs are equally as 'unsuitable' as those who clearly fall short of your requirements. Thus you are aiming to achieve:

the right person for the job

and

the right job for the person

So, assuming that our job offer has been accepted, we shall now move on to consider briefly the induction and evaluation processes for our new employee before summing up the role of the personnel practitioner.

INDUCTION

Successful organisations will ensure that this process is treated as an important activity and has sufficient resources devoted to it. The main reason is that new employees who have undergone an effective induction programme are likely to be competent performers at their jobs more quickly than those whose induction was scanty or non-existent. Also the former group are less likely to leave the organisation at an early stage than the latter group (this phenomenon is commonly known as the 'induction crisis' and signifies a dissatisfaction with the job or the organisation or both).

Different employees have different requirements, but they are all likely to need:

- to learn new tasks and procedures
- initial direction
- to make contacts and begin to develop relationships
- to understand the organisational culture
- to feel accepted.

There are, however, certain groups of employees who may need special consideration eg:

- school and college leavers
- women returning to work
- disabled employees
- management trainees
- members of minority ethnic groups
- employees who have undergone internal transfer or promotion.

As an example, the first group listed will know very little about the working environment. With more experienced recruits, you can provide basic information and then ask them what else they want to know. You cannot rely on school or college leavers in the same way, because 'They don't know what they don't know'! (The ACAS Advisory Booklet No. 7, *Induction of new employees*, provides guidance on these special needs and how they can be accommodated.)

The commencement of the induction process is difficult to pinpoint because, for employees new to the organisation, the imparting of information begins with the job advertisement. We could therefore argue that the process starts at this early stage and plan accordingly. Usually, however, when designing an induction programme, we start with the first day of employment and then timetable activities to be included over the first few weeks.

Induction programmes vary between two extremes: the simple check-list approach (to cover the essential information that an employee must be told) to comprehensive induction packages (which include, for example, video messages from the chief executive, guest speakers, 'getting to know you' exercises, and group activities). The check-list approach is likely to be brief, take place at the workstation, and involve the new employee and his or her immediate supervisor only (possibly with the participation of a representative of the personnel department or the health and safety officer, or both). The second, more sophisticated (and more costly) approach is likely to take place away from the workplace and involve more people at a senior level in the organisation. Also, in accordance with economies of scale, organisations are inclined to provide this programme periodically only, ie when there are sufficient numbers of new employees who can attend. Neither of these two extreme approaches is preferable to the other: their worth is gauged on how successful they are in helping the new employee to settle down quickly and become effective in the job.

Finally, let's consider the information that should be provided. As a minimum, employees should be informed about:

• the organisation's background and structure

• the organisation's products, services, and markets

• the conditions of employment eg pay, hours of work, holidays, sick pay, pension scheme

• the organisation's rules and procedures

• the physical layout of the organisation

• health and safety issues (NB it is crucial that these are covered in the very early stages of employment)

• first aid arrangements

• employee involvement and communication arrangements

• trade union arrangements (if any)

• welfare and employee benefits and facilities.

EVALUATION

As with the majority of activities that personnel practitioners become involved with, there is a strong argument for evaluating the success of your recruitment and selection procedures. This is, however, not just a simple matter of concluding that, for instance, an advertisement for a clerical officer's post was successful because 250 applications were received. In fact, it is likely that the reverse is true, because sifting through 250 application forms will have been a time-consuming and costly exercise. Every stage of the recruitment and selection process should be reviewed to see whether mistakes were made and whether a repetition of them can be avoided in the future.

It would be good practice to consider the following questions, but note that some may be more appropriately addressed or re-addressed in three, six or twelve months' time:

1 Did you get the job analysis stage right? That is:

• Did you carry out a thorough field study?

• Is the job description an accurate reflection of the range and type of activities and the level of responsibility involved?

- Are the personnel specification requirements defined in specific and measurable terms?

- Are there any important omissions or unnecessary inclusions in the personnel specification?

- Was a new recruit justified or should the work have been organised differently?

2 Did you get the advertising stage right? That is:

- Did the advert give sufficient information about the job and the person required to encourage suitable applicants only?

- Was the advertisement eye-catching?

- Did you choose the most appropriate media?

- Did you get the timing right?

- Have you carried out an analysis to see which media produced the most cost-effective results?

3 Did you get the selection stage right? That is:

- Did you choose the most appropriate methods for selection?

- Did you ensure that the information generated by each method was cross-checked for validity?

- Did you ensure that only relevant information was considered in decision-making?

- Have you carried out an analysis to see which of the methods used were the most fruitful and cost-effective?

4 Did you get the induction stage right? That is:

- Did the induction programme run smoothly?

- Was the employee properly assisted to settle in and quickly learn the job?

- How much did the induction process cost?

5 Did you select the right person? That is:

- Did the employee become effective as quickly as expected?

- Did the employee require more assistance, training, or support than expected?

- Is the employee still in the post and performing at a satisfactory level?

- Has the employee made satisfactory progress regarding salary reviews or promotion?

6 Did you ensure compliance at all stages with equal opportunities legislation?

7 What would you do differently next time?

Let's return to our example at the beginning of this section of the advertisement for a clerical officer's post. It is tempting to blame the high level of unemployment in the locality for the overwhelming response, but it is quite likely that the job advertisement was too vague in stipulating the essential requirements. Thus potential candidates were not encouraged to deselect themselves from the process and it was necessary to plough through all 250 application forms to see which candidates were really suitable for short-listing. Thus the person responsible for the poor drafting of the advertisement has not only wasted the time of all those involved in the recruitment and selection process (and organisational money) but has also falsely raised the hopes of a large number of unsuitable candidates.

Having considered this important but often forgotten issue of evaluation, we shall now summarise the many roles played by personnel practitioners in carrying out the activities associated with the recruitment and selection of staff.

THE ROLE OF PERSONNEL PRACTITIONERS

In considering the activities above we have touched on a number of the roles performed by personnel practitioners at various stages of the recruitment and selection process:

An advisory role to line managers
It is rare for all of the above activities to be performed solely by personnel practitioners. In any event, it is generally wise to include line managers at the job analysis stage because of their specialist knowledge, and at the selection stage so that they have played a part in selecting their own member of staff and will therefore be more likely to be committed to the new employee's success (and so that you will not get all of the blame for a poor decision!). Following on from this, it is worth noting that an interview panel commonly consists of the line manager and a personnel practitioner. This may involve you in an *influencing* role when, say, the line manager is tempted to offer the post to a candidate for subjective reasons (eg the manager and candidate attended the same school) rather than objective reasons (ie ones linked to the personnel specification).

An administrative role
This is to ensure that information is sought, chased, and checked, that appropriate records are kept, and that all interested parties are kept in touch with the timetable of events.

A training or educational role
There may also be a *policing* role to ensure that equal opportunities principles and policies are adhered to at all stages of the process.

A public relations role
This arises owing to the need to attract suitable candidates and involves conveying information about the job, the person required, and the organisation itself. Also, the way in which candidates are dealt with in making enquiries, pursuing applications, and attending interviews may confirm or contradict their first impressions of the organisation.

An assessment role
Finally, personnel practitioners play a role in assessing candidates by interviewing, observing, testing, and evaluating them using a range of selection methods.

SUMMARY

You should by now be familiar with the key issues involved in the recruitment and selection of staff. We have looked at why recruitment and selection are important (regardless of the economic climate), the relevant legislation, the various stages involved, the importance of the induction and evaluation processes, and the various roles played by personnel practitioners.

You should note that even if your experience of recruitment and selection is limited, it is likely that you will have applied for at least one position for which you were granted an interview. Thus, if you are unfamiliar with the whole process from the viewpoint of the interviewer, you will be familiar with it from the interviewee's perspective. Nothing can replace the experience of actually conducting your first interview, but you are likely to have an opinion on the good and bad practices that you observed while being interviewed. Reflect on such experiences to ensure that you do not make the same mistakes that others may have made. Continue this learning process by attempting the activities listed below before moving on to the next chapter.

Finally, please note that a list of legislative acts and codes, further reading, and recommended video titles is provided at the end of this chapter.

ACTIVITIES

1 Consider the example of a poor advertisement given on page 55. Redesign the advertisement so that it complies with the AIDA guidelines and make proposals for the timing and placing of the advertisement in the media of your choice. Justify your choice and find out how much it would cost. Discuss the drafting of your advertisement with one or more of your learning sources.

2 Look at a number of job advertisements in a local or national newspaper and pick out two examples: one good and the other poor. Think about the reasons for your decision. Consider where (and when) you found the advertisements, how eye-catching and professional they look, the image they portray of the organisation, whether they provide enough information for potential applicants etc. Do the advertisements comply with the guidelines provided by the mnemonic AIDA? What advice would you give the people responsible for the poor example on how to improve the effectiveness of their advertising in the future?

3 Taking into account best practice, study your own job description and personnel specification (if they exist) and draft out accurate, up-to-date, and comprehensive versions after carrying out a systematic analysis. Discuss their contents with one or more of your learning sources. You will be surprised at how much you do!

4 Look back at a recent vacancy within your organisation and analyse the process of recruiting and selecting the successful candidate by answering the following questions:

• Was an appropriate choice of advertising media made?

• Was an appropriate choice of selection methods made?

- What lessons have been learned and what suggestions do you have for improvements in the event of similar vacancies arising in the future?

5 Using the same example as for activity number 4, analyse the induction programme carried out when the successful candidate took up his or her post (this exercise can still be applicable if the successful candidate was an internal one). What suggestions do you have for improvements in the induction process for the future?

6 Having studied the section above on evaluation, consider which methods are currently employed by your organisation to evaluate the success or otherwise of the recruitment and selection process. Suggest two or three major improvements. Put these down in the form of an action plan with, if possible, time-scales and the names of persons responsible.

REFERENCES AND FURTHER READING

The following three booklets are available from the Advisory, Conciliation and Arbitration Service (ACAS), ACAS Reader Ltd, P.O. Box 16, Earl Shilton, Leicester, LE9 8ZZ; tel. 01455 852 225:

Advisory booklet on recruitment and selection of new employees. (Undated) Leicester, ACAS.

Advisory booklet on employment policies. (Undated) Leicester, ACAS.

Advisory booklet on induction of new employees. (Undated) Leicester, ACAS.

Courtis J. (1994) *Recruitment advertising: right first time.* London, Institute of Personnel and Development.

The following two publications are available from Croner Publications Ltd, Croner House, London Road, Kingston-upon-Thames, Surrey, KT2 6SR; tel. 0181 547 3465:

Croner's personnel assistant's handbook. Kingston-upon-Thames, Croner Publications.

Croner's reference book for employers. Kingston-upon-Thames, Croner Publications.

Fowler A. (1990) 'How to write a job advertisement'. *People Management Plus.* October. pp31–2.

Hackett P. (1995) *The selection interview.* London, Institute of Personnel and Development.

Woodruffe C. (1994) *Assessment centres: identifying and developing competence.* London, Institute of Personnel and Development.

See also the following, available from the Communications Department of the Institute of Personnel and Development (IPD), IPD House, Camp Road, London SW19 4UX); tel. 0181 971 9000:

IPD key facts on age and employment. London, Institute of Personnel and Development.

IPD key facts on harassment at work. London, Institute of Personnel and Development.

See also:

IPD guide on recruitment. (1996) London, Institute of Personnel and Development.

IPD guide on psychological testing. (1996) London, Institute of Personnel and Development.

ACTS OF PARLIAMENT AND CODES OF PRACTICE

Disability Discrimination Act 1995

Race Relations Act 1976

Sex Discrimination Acts 1975 and 1986

The following is available from the Commission for Racial Equality, Elliot House, 10–12 Allington Street, London, SW1E 5EH; tel. 0171 404 1213:

Code of practice: for the elimination of racial discrimination and the promotion of equality of opportunity in employment. (1984) London, CRE.

The following is available from HMSO Publications Centre (mail, fax, and telephone orders only), P.O. Box 276, London, SW8 5DT; tel. 0171 404 1213:

Code of practice: for the elimination of discrimination in the field of employment against disabled persons or persons who have had a disability. (1996) London, HMSO.

The following is available from the Equal Opportunities Commission (EOC), Overseas House, Quay Street, Manchester M3 3HN; tel. 0161 833 9244:

Code of practice: for the elimination of discrimination on the grounds of sex or marriage and the promotion of equality of opportunity in employment. (1984) Manchester, EOC.

VIDEOS

It's your choice. (1993) Video Arts (selecting candidates).

More than a gut feeling. (1988) Melrose.

When can you start? (1988) Video Arts (attracting candidates).

5 Training and development

INTRODUCTION

Training is a process through which individuals are helped to learn a skill or technique. The skill may be primarily manual, as in using a keyboard, or essentially intellectual, such as negotiating a house sale. The latter are often referred to as 'soft skills' since no 'hard' equipment is involved. Instruction is a very typical form of training, but there are many others. There is often an end-point, perhaps the achievement of a specific data-entry speed.

Development places emphasis on the growth of the individual. It relates to acquiring a very broad range of soft skills through planned activities and experience. Management of people, handling work relationships, and leadership are typical of broad ranges of skills that are *developed*. Success in all these areas requires maturity of judgement. There is no fixed end-point to development, because individuals can continually improve, for example, their leadership skills.

The structure of this chapter follows the steps in the 'training cycle' which we shall look at in a moment. First, though, we consider the importance of training and development activities.

WHY ARE THEY IMPORTANT?

We shall be looking at the unrelenting pace of change in the world and at its implications for training needs. If our organisations respond to change early, they will prosper and gain rewards in terms of security, profit, or attainment of their goals. Today commercial products can be imitated, some almost immediately. So technological advantage may give one producer an 'edge' over others, but these other producers can catch up quickly. In a free market economy all organisations have similar access to capital, to customers, and to employees. It is their effectiveness in operating, as organisations of people, that primarily distinguishes one from another. Key factors in operating effectively are the knowledge and skills of people.

In the commercial world, then, if we train our people and continually ensure they have up-to-date knowledge and up-to-date skills, it follows that we shall able to compete effectively, and reasonably expect to prosper. Few, if any, jobs today are protected from commercial realities. Even those not originally seen as being commercial organisations, for example charities, now place considerable importance on obtaining well-trained professional people to run their operations.

As a personnel practitioner you have an important role to play. You should be able to relate to commercial needs and your corporate mission, using them to help identify suitable training. Training and development, like every other operation, requires to be managed. Personnel practitioners need to acquire advanced skills and knowledge to do so effectively.

We shall commence with a look at the training cycle, which helps identify the main principles involved in managing training and development activities.

THE TRAINING CYCLE

Figure 2 The training cycle

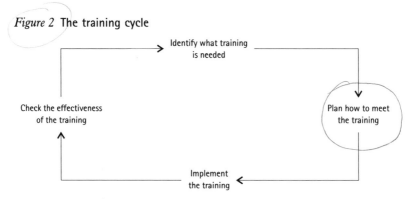

Figure 2 describes how training is managed. It is a continuous cycle. We shall look first at how training needs are identified, usually referred to as 'training needs analysis'. Then we shall look at how to plan a training programme, highlighting the ingredients available to satisfy those needs that have been identified. When training is designed and implemented, we need to be aware of the different learning styles that individuals prefer, and we shall look at the four styles. Last, and not least, we shall look at how the effectiveness of training can be evaluated.

British Governments have recognised the need for training if Britain is to compete internationally. They have developed and supported initiatives to encourage employers and employees to take responsibility for training. One of these initiatives is the Investors in People (IIP) award given to organisations that can show they are truly investing in their people, ie increasing their skills and knowledge towards corporate objectives. So it is worth looking at the four IIP principles. Organisations that can demonstrate their ability to satisfy these principles can display the prestigious IIP insignia on their letterhead and at their premises. The principles are interesting, because you will see similarities between them and the training cycle.

Investors in People principles

Principle One: Commitment

An *Investor in People* makes a commitment from the top to develop all employees to achieve its business objectives.

Principle Two: Planning

An *Investor in People* regularly reviews the needs and plans the training and development of all employees.

Principle Three: Action

An *Investor in People* takes action to train and develop individuals on recruitment and throughout their employment.

Principle Four: Evaluation

An *Investor in People* evaluates the investment in training and development to assess achievement and improve future effectiveness.

© Investors in People UK 1996

Although training is a continuous cycle, we shall look first at how training needs arise.

TRAINING NEEDS ARISE BECAUSE THE WORLD CHANGES

Change is continuous; it affects the environment in which organisations operate; and it exists within organisations themselves. Employees are affected by change and they must adapt, learn new skills, cope with different pressures, acquire new knowledge, and forge new relationships. Training brings additional resources to individuals to enable them to change and develop. When we looked at the role of the personnel practitioner (Chapter 2) we briefly identified the types of changes that affect the corporate environment. We shall now examine these in more detail and relate them to training and development.

- In recent years *political* change has brought about the need for a wider range of management skills in many parts of the public sector. This change has created new challenges for managers who previously had little control over their finances, employment practices, marketing, or ability to exploit opportunities. Examples of these changes are privatisation, competitive tendering for services, and the move of further education establishments out of local government control and into individual corporate bodies. Politicians also seek to influence the participation of organisations and individuals in training. This has led to initiatives such as IIP Awards, National Vocational Qualifications (NVQs), and National Training Awards (NTAs).

- The *economic* conditions of the early 1990s caused many companies to restructure, thus cutting out layers of management, closing operations, and losing experienced staff. The wider responsibilities of the remaining staff and the loss of experienced employees create the need for greater skills, particularly in the managerial and supervisory areas.

- *Social* change creates training needs. For example, as more people travel abroad and experience the high levels of customer service in North America and the Far East they become more demanding in their expectations for customer service at home. As a further example, in society we now acknowledge women's right to occupy jobs at the highest levels in companies and institutions. Both these examples indicate the need for training, the first in customer care skills and the second in management skills for women (to help redress the imbalance at senior levels).

- *Technological* change is relentless. The training needs it creates in computer skills, in advanced technical skills, and simply in new ways of doing things are widespread and substantial. Technology also provides many new techniques for trainers to use in the process of training itself.

- The *law* changes continually as well, and personnel practitioners are only too aware of the training needs it creates for them. Keep in mind that employment is only one area affected by the law. Product liability, labelling of consumer goods, and regulation of financial services are just a few examples where the law creates training needs for employers.

- The *environment* changes too. Britain's drought of 1995–6 brought a new set of challenges for the newly privatised water companies. In many industries, pollution can be reduced by better training of operatives. (The list continues.)

These changes lead to new products, services, and standards of expected performance that, in turn, demand new skills and abilities. Organisations that can respond to these changes quickly by training their employees appropriately steal an advantage over their competitors.

Listening to and reading suitable media material will raise your awareness of the corporate environment. We recommend:

- *People Management*

- other training publications

- quality daily or Sunday newspapers

- quality magazines covering business or current affairs

- BBC Radio 4

- the Internet.

Individual training needs also arise internally, directly or indirectly, as a result of external changes. Even without those external changes, training needs will arise for employees who are new to the organisation, gain promotion, relocate, are redeployed, or are due to retire. So, when looking at training needs, we have to consider not only changes in the environment but also changes for individuals.

TRAINING NEEDS ARISE BECAUSE PEOPLE'S JOBS AND CAREERS CHANGE

Induction training addresses the needs of new-starters, and similar training is needed for all employees who transfer or are promoted within the organisation. Some special cases are considered below.

- School leavers have much to learn about the world of work. They need to understand the level of commitment required and to be able to assess others' expectations of them. Working *with* adults will be a novel experience, and new attitudes need to be formed. All this is quite apart from the actual mechanics of doing the job. Comparatively simple everyday tasks, such as answering the telephone, can be a major source of anxiety to those who have never been in employment before. (Perhaps you can remember your first day at work!)

- Young graduates, especially those who have not been in employment before, need similar induction to that for school leavers, although they can be expected to learn faster. Most employers give special consideration to graduates, recognising that they may eventually become senior managers in the organisation. Building relationships with people in many departments of the organisation and having a broad understanding of what each function does is critical for those who seek a progressive career. Graduate training schemes invariably recognise this, and graduates often spend time in different functions before settling into their chosen career path.

- New employees who already have experience elsewhere need to learn about the culture of your organisation, ie how 'things are done'. They need to meet, and begin to build relationships with, those with whom they will be in regular contact. Systems and routines will be different from those of their previous employer. At the same time, new employees usually bring alternative approaches that can benefit their new employer.

- Returners from maternity leave, a career break, or a period of unemployment need time and help to build up their confidence. Often there will be new and unfamiliar technology, and perhaps a new working climate with new or different expectations. Teaching provides an example, in which the Education Reform Act 1988 and local management of schools have created a very different climate in the 1990s from that which existed in the 1980s. Given support to adapt and training in new skills, returners usually regain their confidence rapidly.

- Employees who have moved from other departments, functions, and sites also need time to acclimatise to their new situations. The building of new relationships and finding the right contacts can be encouraged by team-building events and by deliberate inclusion in social activities.

Providing mentors and associates to aid all these transitions is a popular way to assist employees. Mentors, usually more senior than the employee, can provide encouragement and support and pass on their own skills and experience as well as leading by example. Associates may be peers of the employee, such as a graduate who joined with the last intake and who can relate easily to a new graduate entrant.

- Retirement calls for a new set of life skills, and responsible employers recognise the need for training for this. They provide preparatory courses covering subjects such as health and financial planning, as well as introducing employees to pensioners' groups.

- Current employees who are not performing at the right level require specific diagnosis. The problem may lie in a lack of technical skills or in attitude, but very often other factors not directly related to training needs may be diagnosed.

- Promotion creates training needs. Surprisingly this is often not recognised. It does not follow that the best operative can become an effective supervisor, that the best salesman is a natural manager, or that an experienced schoolteacher knows how to be a headteacher. The Peter Principle, which suggests that everyone is promoted to their level of incompetence, possibly reflects the lack of training that most employees receive on promotion.

- Future potential is another reason for training and developing individuals. It particularly relates to those who are progressing to managerial or professional careers, where the responsibility for development of skills rests more heavily with the individual. 'Fast-tracking' is the term used when individuals are identified as having significant future potential. Such individuals are singled out for special development. Activities may include studying for professional qualifications, secondments to other sites, departments, or companies, special project responsibilities, and mentoring from one or more senior managers.

LEVELS OF TRAINING NEEDS ANALYSIS

When we look at the above issue we shall see that training is needed at three levels. These are the organisation, the job or occupation, and the individual employee.

The organisation
Customer care is typical of a training need that originates at the level of the organisation. It could arise from a board-level decision to change the organisation's image in this one regard.

Job or occupation
Training in electronic 'point of sales' equipment (eg the scanners familiar at supermarket checkouts) is an example of training that will apply to everyone in a specific job – in this case, checkout operators.

Individual employee
Here there may be an opportunity for training where an individual has a particular need or the organisation requires an individual to be trained in a particular area. For the personnel officer, an employment law course or secondment to another organisation might be examples.

MAKING TRAINING NEEDS ANALYSIS COMPREHENSIVE

Jill Fairbairns has provided a model that emphasises three matters that need to be addressed in making decisions about appropriate training. We shall use this model to describe our approach to identifying where training should be concentrated. In part, it links the three levels above but it can also be applied to evaluating the suitability of training solutions at each level.

Throughout our working lives we increase our levels of knowledge and skills in order to perform work activities well. The acquisition of relevant knowledge and skills opens up opportunities to individuals for increased job performance, career development, and personal development. Organisations continually seek the best return on their limited funds so it is necessary to be selective and to identify those areas that will be important in the particular job in question (important in my job – see Figure 3).

Most jobs today need a wide range of skills and knowledge: some are critical and others desirable for top performance. Job-holders usually have the majority of those skills and knowledge already but, for the reasons outlined above, there will always be areas that can benefit from additional training (in need of training – see Figure 3). So at this point we would be looking for the overlap between importance in the job and need of training.

Figure 3 Factors in the selection of training (Fairbairns' model)

The third factor involves the culture of the organisation. We looked at culture in Chapter 2 and observed that businesses are characterised by different attitudes and priorities, ie the corporate culture. Training for knowledge and skills that do not fit comfortably with the *corporate culture* will either put the trained person at odds with that culture or, more probably, lead to the training being rejected on the basis that 'it does not work here'. One example of a cultural factor is the attitude to NVQs or Scottish Vocational Qualifications (SVQs); some organisations are more enthusiastic about these than others. In an enthusiastic organisation an NVQ initiative will receive a better reception and more support from senior managers. Identifying the cultural direction in which your organisation is going will help identify the most relevant training (likely to be encouraged and rewarded – see Figure 3).

Personnel practitioners will benefit from taking these three factors into account in selecting suitable training activities. It is where such activities address the overlap between all three factors that the most benefits are likely to be realised (again, see Figure 3).

The person being trained is a further factor to be considered. Offering training can imply weakness or that an individual has a problem with some aspect of his or her performance. Unless individuals see training as an opportunity or believe it is important in their jobs and relevant to their organisation, then they are likely to reject it. So individuals should be involved in the plans for their training to encourage their commitment to it.

GATHERING THE INFORMATION

To carry out a training needs analysis for your organisation you will need information that can be evaluated against the factors mentioned above. The information must relate to the level at which you are doing your analysis: organisation, occupation, or employee. Suitable source material for the analysis is likely to include some of the following:

- mission and values (formal culture)
- business plans

- succession plans

- views and observations about 'how we do things around here' (this is the informal culture, not necessarily the same as the formal culture)

- appraisal records

- evidence of competence for individuals (eg portfolios)

- opportunities for improvement (eg development opportunities)

- minutes of meetings (eg action points that highlight needs)

- questionnaires

- job descriptions

- performance targets

- observation of employees at work

- relevant NVQs or SVQs

- interviews with:

  - managers

  - staff

  - subordinates

  - internal customers

  - external customers.

Using sources such as these is important because you start with the needs that relate to the business. Once you know what is needed, then you can start to consider the best way to meet those needs.

When you have gathered the source material and feel well informed, it is time to carry out your analysis. This could be at the level of the organisation, job, or individual. To illustrate the process we shall consider examples at the job level.

You need to ask what job performance is needed in the particular situation. The answer should be in the form of a level of performance or standard of competence. For instance, a management meeting may have decided that all telephone calls are to be answered politely, competently, and effectively. Another way of defining the required performance may be to use an NVQ/SVQ standard that directly defines the competence – for example, to select candidates for jobs within agreed time-scales and budgets.

We shall assume that in these examples training is a suitable remedy. That may not be the case in all circumstances; for example, if operations are underresourced then training is an inappropriate solution.

Next you need to ascertain what performance or competence is being achieved at present. Perhaps callers are kept waiting for a reply with no apology offered when the call is answered. Maybe the person answering does not understand how to handle some of the enquiries, or incomplete messages are taken. In the second example, selection of candidates may regularly overrun both time-scales and budgets. The difference between this and the level of performance needed is known as the 'training gap'.

You may have to try to estimate what that 'gap' is *costing* the organisation, or the gain and benefits of closing that gap. We may be able to get information about sales lost owing to poor telephone technique, or estimate the costs of taking an extra day to fill a vacancy. This is important because these costs will provide the justification for the training costs or, perhaps, lead to the conclusion that training is not justified in a particular instance.

The next phase is to plan the training and development.

TRAINING AND DEVELOPMENT PLANS

Here a balancing act is required between available resources, which may be influenced by the benefits that have been estimated, and the identified needs. Achieving such a balance is a matter of skill. As we saw in the Fairbairns' model (Figure 3), you will have to weigh up needs in the context of the political considerations, style, and culture of the organisation.

Let's look at some of the factors that will have to be considered.

The internal training and development resources available
You must understand the size of the training budget and how it is structured. Structure can be important; for example, some budgets may apply only to amounts invoiced; thus the use of a supervisor to train tele-enquiry operators may well not be counted against such budgets. This does not mean that using the supervisor would be without cost, but it may save some of the training budget for use elsewhere.

Investigate the availability of grants and subsidies for internal training from Training and Enterprise Councils (TECs) or Local Enterprise Companies in Scotland (LECs), Business Links, and other sources. At the same time we should assess the requirements placed on the organisation by such bodies as a condition of providing grants or subsidies. For example, you might be expected to train your personnel administrator to an NVQ/SVQ standard and to train your personnel officer as an assessor.

You may have some facilities available internally, such as a training centre well equipped for craft training, management training, computer training, or for all of these. On the other hand, there may be very limited facilities. Nonetheless, in most cases there will be equipment available that could be used for training. Production departments, for example, may have idle production lines that could be used for training purposes. Setting up a small office for tele-enquiry training may be straightforward.

Consider the availability and capability of training specialists and trainers within the company. These may be increased by training supervisors in instruction, for example. In addition, experienced employees may be available for training-based activities. At more senior levels, experienced managers may be willing to coach or mentor more junior managers or staff. This can be a valuable *development* activity for both the senior and the junior.

Another valuable development activity is secondment to another section, site, or associated company. Equally, these locations and jobs themselves may provide project opportunities. A local non-competitor may have a good tele-enquiry operation and be willing to share expertise. Some organisations are very innovative and engage in formal partnership arrangements, sometimes including a training provider, to share employee development opportunities.

The external training and development resources available
Using external resources invariably has an opportunity cost. There will be absence from the workplace and, in consequence, temporary loss of production, sales, service, or contribution to the business. Often these costs are 'hidden' in that they do not appear in any financial calculations, but they are there nonetheless. In addition, there will be the cost of course fees, travel, and accommodation. Such costs are rarely hidden and are likely to need justification. If there are grants or subsidies available, these may help. Again, you need to know the conditions laid down by the bodies providing them. Expect questions as to whether the external resources are in fact available internally or could be more economically provided internally. Investigate, also, the availability of grants and subsidies for external training from the bodies we mentioned above.

Finally, you need to evaluate the quality of such training, its relevance, and its relationship to the culture of the organisation and to the quality standards demanded in the workplace. A local telephone techniques course might not meet your expectations. You should also consider the relevance of training to an individual's career. Qualifications, in particular, can be relevant to the needs of both the organisation and the individual; we look at these next.

Qualifications
In many organisations it is important to have qualified people; in some cases, third parties may impose such requirements. Hospitals are obvious examples, where qualifications are necessary for doctors and nursing staff. In industry, accountants and engineers are examples of professional people who are frequently required to be suitably qualified. Even when not a statutory requirement, qualifications help to show that responsibilities are taken seriously. Health and safety qualifications, for example, indicate a responsible approach to an important issue, one for which a company may be held liable for injuries and occupational ill-health.

Qualifications provide external verification of skills, competence, or knowledge. This can be helpful, for example, where pay is related to level of qualification.

- *Examination-based qualifications* provide evidence of knowledge and ability to examine issues and solve problems. High performance in examinations may also imply judgement. However, such a guide is not always reliable and, furthermore, examinations rarely assess practical skills.

- *Competence-based qualifications* depend on providing evidence of ability to carry out specific tasks to the standard expected in the workplace. Evidence is assessed by a qualified assessor who judges whether it provides sufficient evidence of competence. Typical evidence might include documents prepared by the 'candidate', reports, copies of correspondence, and witness testimony about carrying out activities to a specified standard. Competence can also be assessed by observation.

- *NVQs and SVQs* are nationally recognised competence qualifications. They provide detailed descriptions (standards) of vocational competencies, breaking them down into units of competence, then into elements of competence. Units of competence can be accredited individually, accumulating into a qualification. Elements of competence describe activities (such as leading a meeting) and have performance criteria against which competence in the activity can be judged (eg handling of conflict). The detailed descriptions can be invaluable in preparing training for specific skills and for checking achievement. TECs, LECs and colleges can help employers identify relevant NVQs/SVQs for their employees.

The use of competence-based workplace training can involve the use of internal advisers and assessors. While these would naturally be supervisors and experienced employees, the cost of training advisers and assessors, of administering the system, and of providing the training may be substantial. One point of caution on competence-based training and NVQs/SVQs: take care not to allow the collection of evidence to develop into a 'paper-chase', because this may obscure the need to develop skills and impart relevant knowledge, ie to help employees to learn – a point we take up now.

CHOOSING APPROPRIATE LEARNING EXPERIENCES

This choice should take into consideration the range of techniques available and individual learning styles.

Training and development techniques

There is a temptation to associate 'training' with the provision of 'training courses'. In practice the majority of learning takes place outside such courses, and is often left to chance. Learning opportunities abound and the training specialist should seek to manage these as effectively as possible. So 'training and development techniques' include using naturally occurring or deliberately created learning opportunities. The examples of techniques and opportunities that we list here can also help you to address your own training and development needs. We return to this list in the activities we suggest in Chapter 9.

On the job

- Job instruction

- Discovery learning

- Coaching

- Work diaries and log books

- Records of continuing professional development

- Job rotation

- Job enlargement

- Job enrichment

- Group meetings

- Projects and assignments

- NVQ/SVQ programmes.

and workshops

d presentations

recording

d reading

ussion groups

- Case-studies

- Role play

- Business games

- Feedback on achievement in presentations, role play, video, etc

- Programmed learning in books, computers, interactive video, and CD-ROM

- Computer simulation

- Assignments

- Action learning

- Outdoor development training.

Learning styles

In choosing appropriate experiences we need to acknowledge that individuals are different. In particular they learn in different ways. Honey and Mumford (see References and Further Reading at the end of this chapter) describe four learning styles that enable individuals to be categorised by their preferred approaches to learning. We have summarised these styles as follows:

Activists   Their approach to learning is very open-minded.
They thrive on activity and tend to decide first and learn afterwards.
They learn best from short 'here and now' exercises eg business games, group work.

Reflectors   They gather and reflect on all available information before making a decision.
They take account of the wider picture.
They prefer to stand back, listen, observe, and record information, eg diaries, time logs.

Theorists   They think problems through in a logical, step-by-step way.
Their decisions tend to be 'black and white' ie categorical.
They use models, systems, concepts, and theories eg conventional science teaching.

Pragmatists They are keen on practical approaches and on solving problems.
They are down to earth – 'If it works, it works.'
They seek to establish a close link between the subject matter and its practical application eg projects, workplace training.

For individuals, it is valuable to play to strong learning styles, although it is also useful to seek to develop the other learning styles. Groups of individuals may benefit from emphasis on a particular style, too: a group of supervisors is more likely to respond to a pragmatic approach, whereas a group of young science graduates would probably respond better to a theoretical approach. In choosing appropriate learning techniques and opportunities you should consider the preferences of the individuals. Training that centres around a number of individuals will have to accommodate a variety of activities to cover the different styles of the participants.

IMPLEMENTING TRAINING ACTIVITIES

The key to successful training activities is planning and preparation. In planning, it is helpful if you can regard people at events as participants in a learning process. Use of terms such as 'attenders', 'trainees', or even 'students' implies they are passive rather than actively involved in a process for which they have responsibility. Carefully consider each of the following:

- the objectives of the event (these can be broad or very specific)
- how many will be trained at any one time
- the length of your learning sessions and how much will be learnt at each session
- how much time is available and how you will divide it up
- the likely preferred learning styles of participants
- the range of training techniques available and their suitability
- how to involve participants in the learning process
- the pace of learning.

If you plan to run a workshop, seminar, or training course you will also have to consider:

- the practical arrangements – room, layout etc
- the use of support material – handouts, videos, visual aids
- the training resources – flip chart, video tape recorder (know how to use it!), overhead projector etc.

When we have implemented our training there is one more task. It is not really the last task, because it is only one step in the training cycle. It is appropriate for it to lead to identification of further needs.

WHY SHOULD WE EVALUATE OUR TRAINING?

It is important to remember that training and development activities are not ends in themselves. The nineteenth-century biologist T. H. Huxley said: 'The great end in life is not knowledge but action.' Unless our activities result in some positive changes in the performance of our organisation, they have no relevant value. Therefore we should evaluate the action that results from our training, if we are to know whether it was worthwhile.

ill have noticed the emphasis placed on evaluation when we
dered the IIP principles earlier in this chapter. It is good practice to
uate any business investment to learn lessons for the future. When we
k at training, some particular reasons to consider are:

- justifying the expense

- providing feedback to the trainer

- providing feedback on techniques

- establishing whether the needs and objectives of the training have been met

- improving future programmes

- identifying further needs

- providing data for justifying further expenditure

- helping top management understand the broad costs and benefits of developing people.

We might be prompted to ask the question posed in the next heading.

Why is training and development so frequently not evaluated?
Looking at the answers to this question helps to identify the practical problems.

- The benefits of training and development are often intangible: effectiveness may improve, but in ways that are not immediately obvious. Development activities help an individual to grow, to improve their judgement, and to increase their value to an employer. Such skill develops gradually and may not become suddenly apparent on completion of the activities.

- Sometimes the objectives of the training have not been defined or, when they have, it may be difficult to measure whether they have been achieved.

- Even where measurable change exists, it is not always easy to establish a direct link between the training and the results, because there are many other factors that may impinge on the same changes.

The result is that evaluation is often confined to questionnaires completed by trainees at the end of a training course. Notwithstanding that courses are only one form of training activity, there are some reasons to be cautious in attaching too much importance to such questionnaires. Easterby-Smith and Tanton (1985) point out three drawbacks:

Evaluations can be conservative:
This is because of:

- the personal investment made by trainers and their understandable anxiety about criticism

- the mutual interests of trainers and trainees in perpetuating a course

- the danger of adverse criticism reflecting on a trainee

Evaluations can be counter-productive
This is because:

- they focus on what trainees want rather than what they need

- they encourage tutors to adopt styles that meet approval rather than being geared to meeting objectives

Inaccuracies may arise
This is because:

- questionnaires are designed to look fair

- participants who feel aggrieved in one way respond in another.

It is worth noting that the fourth IIP principle states that an Investor in People evaluates the investment in training and development to *assess achievement and improve future effectiveness*. This implies that we do need to look at training beyond the level of course questionnaires.

What we find particularly helpful in evaluating the effectiveness of training is a model proposed by Hamblin and described by Reid and Barrington (1997: 344) – see Table 6, in which there are examples of measures for assessing the true value of training at each of five levels.

Table 6 Hamblin's levels of evaluation

The levels		Methods of evaluation
Level 1 Reactions of the trainees – to the content and methods of training, to the trainer, and to any other factors perceived as relevant. What the trainee thought about the training.		Discussion Interviews Questionnaires Recommendations of trainees Desire for further training
Level 2 Learning attained during the learning period. Did the trainees learn what was intended?	*Behaviour* *Knowledge and* *understanding* *Skills* *Attitude*	Objectives attained Examinations and other tests Analysis by observation of demonstrated skill Evidence of skills applied Projects or assignments Questionnaires
Level 3 Job behaviour in the work environment at the end of the training period. Did the learning get transferred to the job?		Production rate Customer complaints Discuss with manager/subordinates/peers Activity-sampling Self-recording of specific incidents Evidence of competence Appraisal
Level 4 Effect on the department. Has the training helped the department's performance?		Minutes of meetings Deadlines met Stress indicators Quality indicators Interview other managers and superiors
Level 5 'The Ultimate Level'. Has the training affected the ultimate well-being of the organisation in terms of business objectives?		Standing of the training officer Growth Quality indicators Stress indicators Achievement of business goals and targets

If, on evaluation, a particular piece of training has achieved its objectives and made a significant contribution to the success of your organisation then you might consider applying for an NTA for your organisation (the awards are competitive). If successful, this accolade would provide substantial publicity: it would publicly recognise your success in following the training cycle.

THE ROLE OF PERSONNEL PRACTITIONERS

Your role in training and development activities will be largely determined by the structure and culture of your organisation. As a personnel practitioner you may be expected to take responsibility for training and development activities. If so, then the content of this chapter will be especially relevant to you.

An influencing role

If you want to influence line managers towards better training decisions then you will benefit by learning to understand their needs. That means talking to them about what they are trying to achieve. You will then be in a position to make positive and helpful suggestions.

By becoming familiar with government initiatives and sources of grant support you will increase your own value and credibility and, hence, your ability to influence.

Remember that many organisations still give training and development low priority. According to Sir John Harvey-Jones (1994), British businesses rarely spend more than 2 per cent of their total payroll budget on training and development, and yet compete with businesses who regard 10–20 per cent as a more appropriate figure. So your most valuable contribution could be to research the value of training and development for your employer and make clear cost-justified cases for improvement.

An administrative role

You take this on when you concentrate on making the arrangements for training and for keeping the records. Significant costs from the precious training budget can be saved by effective arrangements and diligent negotiation. Well-organised records on objectives and outcomes can provide valuable information for evaluating the true benefits of training activities. However, if you want to break out of the administrative mould you should use your learning in this chapter and your unique access to training records to move towards an influencing role.

A training role

This comes into play when you are appointed as a personnel *and* training practitioner. If you are so appointed, you will have clear training responsibilities. If this also involves *delivering* training on a regular basis then you may consider trying to specialise in training or personnel rather than spreading your skills and responsibilities too thinly.

Delivery of training requires planning and thorough preparation. Personnel responsibilities often require you to respond to demands that arise suddenly and unexpectedly. Therefore the two responsibilities do not always sit very comfortably alongside each other.

A decision-making role

Here you have the opportunity to make decisions about training needs, about the response to those needs, and about the effectiveness of the response. This chapter should have given you the basic understanding you require to start making decisions. If you are new to the task, then commence slowly and build up your experience as you go round the training cycle.

An overseeing role

This role requires you to keep in touch with all the training activities in your sphere of responsibility, which will help you to influence others, as we discussed above. You may be able to pick out many ways of improving the relevance and effectiveness of training.

SUMMARY

We have looked at the steps of the training cycle and used those to examine the management of training and development. It is the changes in the environment in which a business operates, and people's job and career changes, that create the need for training.

Training needs can be identified at the level of the organisation, job or occupation, at the individual employee level. We have to consider not just what may require training but whether that is both important in the job and likely to be recognised or rewarded within the culture of the organisation.

Training needs are established by examining the gap between the performance that is sought and the performance currently being achieved. A wide variety of sources is available to help determine both the desired performance and current performance.

In formulating plans for training and development it is important to examine the internal resources available, the external resources, and the relevance of qualifications. We can select from a wide variety of techniques and opportunities and should never restrict our concept of training and development to training courses alone. Individuals have preferences for the ways in which they learn – their learning styles. The choice of training activities should take this into account.

To complete the learning cycle, we emphasised the value of evaluating training, considered some of the practical obstacles, and identified a model that can help structure our evaluation.

If you have the opportunity to be involved in training and development activities, then we suggest you involve yourself with enthusiasm. There is much to be gained.

ACTIVITIES

1 If your organisation is seeking the IIP accolade, you may be asked a number of questions during the process. Try asking some of the typical ones of yourself or of close colleagues:

  • Does your organisation make any statements about its policy on training and development of which you aware? Are you able to name any of these?

- What do you think are your organisation's business objectives?

- How are you able to contribute to them?

- Considering the possible contributions, how do you think you might improve your ability to perform?

- Does anyone discuss your training and development needs with you?

- Are you able to describe any opportunities for training that might exist for you in your organisation?

- If so, do you intend to take, or have you taken, any of these opportunities?

2 Look at the lists of training techniques provided earlier in this chapter. Are any of those listed unfamiliar to you? Discuss any that you are unclear about with a learning source and undertake further reading, as appropriate.

3 Look back at the learning style descriptions. From these you should be able to decide who will benefit most from each of the following activities:

- 'having a go'

- taking a back seat in a meeting

- applying a new technique to a current problem

- an intellectual debate

- keeping a daily log

- being coached by an expert

- exciting experiences

- being cross-examined on a decision they have made.

We are not giving you the answers here but there are two of each style represented above. Activists and pragmatists can be difficult to separate. Remember pragmatists like to have ideas that are (as their name suggests) practical and which they can apply immediately.

4 Evaluation of a training programme, course, or exercise should be measured *against its objectives*. The result of the evaluation may legitimately lead to improved objectives, but the training event itself should be reviewed against the original objectives.

Take a training activity in which you have been involved recently, perhaps a Certificate in Personnel Practice (CPP) programme if you are currently a participant. Investigate the objectives of the activity. Then discuss with others who have followed a similar activity the effectiveness of that activity. Try to decide how that effectiveness might be measured *at your place of work*. Concentrate on Level 3 of Hamblin's model (see Table 6) and, if you feel it appropriate, Level 4 or even 5. Look for some tangible measures, remembering that it is *actions* that really count in the workplace. Relate these back to the objectives in order to make your decision.

FURTHER READING

EASTERBY-SMITH M. *and* TANTON M. (1985) 'Turning course evaluation from an end to a means'. *Personnel Management*. April. pp25–7.

FAIRBURNS J. (1991) 'Plugging the gap in training needs analysis'. *Personnel Management*. February. pp43–5.

HARRISON R. (1992) *Employee development*. London, Institute of Personnel Management.

HARVEY-JONES SIR J. (1994) *All together now*. London, Heinemann.

HONEY P. *and* MUMFORD A. (1992a) *The manual of learning styles*. Maidenhead, Honey.

HONEY P. *and* MUMFORD A. (1992b) *Using your learning styles*. Maidenhead, Honey.

REID M. A. *and* BARRINGTON H. A. (1997) *Training interventions: managing employee development*. 5th ed. London, Institute of Personnel and Development.

Investors in People UK provide a number of publications, in particular:

The Investors in People standard (IIP80a).

How to become an Investor in People (IIP82a).

There is a variety of information available from your local TEC or LEC on NVQs/SVQs. See also the Institute of Personnel and Development's *Training Extras* and *Training Essentials* series, which cover all aspects of the training cycle. In particular see:

BOYDELL T. *and* LEARY M. (1996) *Identifying training needs*. London, Institute of Personnel and Development.

BRAMLEY P. (1996) *Evaluating training*. London, Institute of Personnel and Development.

National Training Awards publish a brochure giving interesting case-studies from award winners. For more information, contact National Training Awards, Room W823, Moorfoot, Sheffield, S1 4PQ (tel. 0345 665 588).

6 Discipline and grievance-handling

INTRODUCTION

Personnel practitioners in larger organisations are likely to recognise and know well only a limited number of the employees in the workplace. Even in smaller organisations contact with employees varies greatly depending on the nature of their roles, their level of seniority etc. Thus personnel practitioners tend to be better acquainted with the employees that they were involved in recruiting, those who attend the same regular meetings (eg shop stewards), and those who are disciplined or who submit grievances. This can result in a somewhat distorted view of the 'typical' employee, because there may be a tendency to assume that employees are always breaching the rules or complaining about their lot. Statistics regarding the incidence of disciplinary action and numbers of grievances submitted will help to put these issues into perspective, as will making the effort to get to know a greater cross-section of employees.

The following chapter sets out to explain against the backdrop of relevant legislation what we mean by disciplinary rules and disciplinary and grievance procedures. (Chapter 3 also provides reference to legislative considerations in this area.) We shall then look at the complex nature of the role of personnel practitioners in discipline and grievance-handling before considering good practice in disciplinary and grievance interviews. The chapter concludes with some suggested activities to develop your knowledge and skills in this important area. First, we shall consider why it is so important that disciplinary incidents and employee grievances are handled with skill and according to laid-down procedures.

WHY ARE THEY IMPORTANT?

Concentrating on discipline first, rules and procedures exist to help employees to improve their performance. They should not be regarded as just a means by which managers can dismiss employees legally. There are several outcomes of poor practice:

• A lax approach to potential disciplinary incidents will lead to an ill-disciplined workforce who do not respect management's authority and are likely to 'play the system' to their own advantage, eg by making their own decisions about working methods and break times. When managers do want to assert their authority by, say, enforcing break times, employees will rightly point to the fact that established custom and practice have overridden written policy and procedure.

- An overenthusiastic use of the disciplinary rules and procedures (often applied in a haphazard and inconsistent way) will lead to employee discontent and is unlikely to be beneficial in realising employee potential and thus maximising productivity.

- Ultimately, management may be faced with a decision to dismiss to an employee. If their reason is insufficient (eg they have overreacted to the incident) or if they act unreasonably in dismissing that employee (eg by failing to follow the procedure correctly) then the chance of the employee making a successful claim of unfair dismissal to an industrial tribunal is increased. Fighting such a claim will be costly and time-consuming and, regardless of the outcome, does little to enhance the reputation of the organisation in the eyes of its employees and outside parties.

Turning now to grievance-handling, procedures exist to enable employees to have a formal means of complaint about their terms and conditions, working environment, and related issues (see the section on grievance-handling regarding the types of issues covered). Failure to encourage use of this system or to respond appropriately to grievances will result in:

- discontent among the workforce because they feel that management are not interested in and do not value their views. This may lead to poor motivation and low productivity.

- missed opportunities to tackle problems at an early stage to ensure that they do not continue, thus creating difficulties for other employees. Ultimately they may escalate into more serious issues, possibly resulting in industrial action.

DISCIPLINE

The legislation relevant to the handling of disciplinary matters (and grievances) is referred to and commented on throughout this chapter. The major piece of relevant legislation is the Employment Rights Act 1996 (ERA). This Act consolidated most of the legislation applicable to the individual rights of employees, including the right not to be unfairly dismissed. All employees will have statutory protection against unfair dismissal after two years' continuous service regardless of the number of hours worked. (NB At the time of writing (June 1997), the requirement of two years' service is subject to challenge in the court system and much discussion in the political arena.)

Obviously, not every disciplinary situation will result in a dismissal, fair or unfair, but personnel practitioners and line managers would be well advised to bear in mind the provisions of ERA, because the manner in which previous disciplinary situations have been handled will be taken into account by industrial tribunals when considering unfair dismissal applications. Let's consider two examples of this:

- A manager who claims that a dismissed employee was previously warned about the consequences of continued poor time-keeping will have to be able to produce the requisite records, the notes of disciplinary interviews, and letters of confirmation to the employee concerned.

- In a case of poor performance, the manager will need to show that he or she reviewed the situation with the employee at regular intervals, sought to help the employee to improve, set realistic targets for improvement, and monitored and kept records of subsequent performance before any decision to dismiss. If the poor performance was due to a change in the job, eg new technology, then the manager should first have considered suitable alternative employment and/or making the employee redundant rather than dismissal. (Chapter 7 stresses the need to ensure that the messages given out to poor performers at formal appraisal interviews do not contradict those issued in the disciplinary context.)

All organisations should have in place written disciplinary and grievance procedures. These form part of the conditions of employment within the organisation. The Advisory, Conciliation and Arbitration Service (ACAS) Code of Practice *Disciplinary practice and procedures in employment* gives guidance to employers on the content and operation of disciplinary rules and procedures and is complemented by the ACAS Advisory Handbook *Discipline at work*, which gives further practical advice. Although it is generally accepted that smaller organisations, ie with fewer than 20 employees, are unlikely to have sophisticated procedures in place, written rules and procedures are strongly recommended (and in a unionised environment, have to have been agreed with the trade union(s)).

Disciplinary rules
We shall deal first with disciplinary rules. These set the standards of behaviour and conduct expected in the workplace. The contents of the rules vary greatly depending on the size of the organisation, the industry, management style, history of employee relations etc. It is likely, however, that they will refer to the following:

- general conduct

- health and safety

- security

- time-keeping and attendance.

Examples of disciplinary rules under each of the above might include:

- Disorderly conduct, threatening behaviour, sky-larking, horseplay, or loitering are strictly forbidden in any part of the works.

- Any defects in personal protective equipment must be reported immediately by the employee to his or her supervisor.

- Employees are strictly forbidden to take from the works any materials, tools, equipment, or other company property unless written permission is first obtained from their departmental manager.

- Under no circumstances is an employee permitted to deface his or her clock card, clock any card other than his or her own, or to tamper with the clocks.

The type of organisation to which these rules might be applicable is not difficult to guess. What do you think – a small retailing outfit, a high-street bank, or a heavy engineering concern?

Disciplinary rules help to ensure a consistent and fair approach to the treatment of employees. Managers obviously wish to have a disciplined workforce, but the majority of employees are likely to be just as keen to have a set of rules in operation so that their working lives can be reasonably orderly. Also, employees want to know what the rules are in order to determine what they should be doing (or not be doing) in order to be successful within the organisation. In fact, in unionised environments it is often forgotten that trade unions also have a common interest with management in promoting standards of conduct. They have two major roles to play:

- to enable members to gain increased *control* over their working lives

- to *represent* members in promoting and protecting their rights.

(See Chapter 3 for more information on the roles played by trade unions in the workplace.)

As a rule of thumb, breaches of disciplinary rules vary in their seriousness. The types of action you should consider are as follows:

- Minor infringements might merit an oral warning (recorded or unrecorded) – eg an occasional late arrival at work.

- More serious infringements might result in a written warning – eg failure to complete quality checks properly.

- Gross misconduct will probably result in summary dismissal (dismissal without notice or pay in lieu of notice) – eg theft, fighting, negligence, or fraud.

You should always point out to an employee that failure to heed warnings by engaging in repeated breaches of the rules, eg continued poor attendance, may ultimately result in dismissal.

It has been mentioned that management must seek to be fair and consistent in applying the disciplinary rules. However, no two disciplinary incidents are ever identical. Thus managers must always ensure that they take into account the circumstances of the case before them. For instance, they are likely to deal less severely with a previously satisfactory employee whose poor attendance is due to temporary domestic commitments than with a short-term employee whose loyalty and commitment are already in some doubt.

It may be that because of a manager's sympathy with the circumstances of an employee's case, that he or she decides that disciplinary action is inappropriate and arranges for counselling to take place (see Figure 4 on page 95). Some may see this as a soft option (putting off the inevitable), but this approach is entirely consistent with the aim of disciplinary rules and procedures, ie to assist employees to improve their performance rather than providing the means for managers to dismiss employees legally.

We shall now consider disciplinary procedures.

Disciplinary procedures
We have seen that where standards of conduct are not met then management may decide to take some form of disciplinary action against the employee(s) concerned. Disciplinary procedures provide guidelines for adherence to the rules and a fair method of dealing with infringements.

The ACAS Code lists the following essential features of disciplinary procedures (the bracketed comments in italics are explanatory ones).

Disciplinary procedures should:

a) be in writing (*if they are not, it will be assumed in industrial tribunal cases that they encompass the ACAS guidelines*)

b) specify to whom they apply (*as there may be different procedures for different groups of employees, eg salaried staff v hourly paid employees*)

c) provide for matters to be dealt with quickly

d) indicate the disciplinary actions that may be taken (*eg oral warning, written warning, final written warning, dismissal, and reference to management discretionary right to suspend an employee with pay in order to carry out a full investigation*)

e) specify the levels of management that have the authority to take the various forms of disciplinary action (*eg first line supervisors may have the authority only to issue oral and written warnings; middle management may be authorised to issue final written warnings; and potential dismissal cases may have to be dealt with by senior managers only*)

f) provide for individuals to be informed of the complaints against them and to be given the opportunity to state their case before decisions are reached (*thus even employees apparently 'caught in the act' should never be instantly dismissed without a proper disciplinary hearing*)

g) give individuals the right to be accompanied by a trade union representative or by a fellow employee of their choice

h) ensure that, except for gross misconduct, no employees are dismissed for a first breach of discipline (*organisations usually provide a list examples of gross misconduct in their disciplinary procedures*)

i) ensure that disciplinary action is not taken until the case has been carefully investigated (*in potential gross misconduct cases, it is generally advisable to suspend the employee concerned on full pay during such investigations; it should be made clear that this is not a punishment in itself – as the saying goes, one is innocent until proven guilty*)

j) ensure that individuals are given an explanation for any penalty imposed (*ie the reason for the decision, the time-scale for which the disciplinary action will remain on the employee's personal record, and the consequences of future breaches of the disciplinary rules*)

k) provide a right of appeal and specify the procedure to be followed (*for example, employees might be required to state that they wish to appeal against a disciplinary decision in writing and submit this to the personnel department within four working days of the disciplinary hearing decision. The appeal would ideally be heard by a manager senior to the one who took the original decision and must be one who has not been involved in the case previously, ie an independent third party. Depending on the size of the organisation, it is possible that only the managing director or chief executive can hear appeals against dismissal decisions*).

The Code also advises that, except for oral warnings, disciplinary actions should be confirmed in writing to the employee concerned. Further, when deciding on the level of disciplinary action (if any), managers should take account of the employee's record and any other relevant factors (often referred to as 'extenuating circumstances').

ACAS is empowered by the Secretary of State for Employment to issue codes of practice such as the one referred to above. Failure to observe the provisions of a code of practice will not of itself render a person liable to any proceedings. However, a code of practice is admissible in evidence in any tribunal proceedings and, if any provision is 'relevant to any questions arising in the proceedings, it shall be taken into account in determining that question'.

The message here is very clear: regardless of the size of your organisation, you should ensure that you incorporate the 'essential features' listed above in your disciplinary procedure. Further, once disciplinary rules and procedures have been formulated in conjunction with interested parties, managers must ensure that the written procedure matches up with the actual practice within the organisation (or employees will have a 'head start' in pursuing their claims to an industrial tribunal).

Failure to follow the correct procedure is one of the commonest arguments put forward (often successfully) by representatives of unfair dismissal applicants. Examples of such failures include:

- an incomplete investigation – eg managers ignoring the evidence of a key witness

- the improper constitution of a disciplinary hearing – eg a supervisor on night-shift making a decision to issue a final written warning when he or she is not authorised to do so

- the absence of a person suitably independent to hear an appeal against a disciplinary decision – eg because the manager who should hear the appeal has been involved in either the investigations or the discussions leading up to the disciplinary decision

- an employee not being accompanied by a representative – eg because the manager assumed that the employee was familiar with this right and would make his or her own arrangements

- an employee not being reminded of the right to appeal and the procedure for so doing (this is an illustration of the importance of keeping accurate notes of all disciplinary hearings so that the validity of such an allegation can be checked).

ERA also states that employers must give new employees written particulars of employment within two months of their starting-date. The written statement must include details of the disciplinary rules and procedure and the grievance procedure (see the later sections on Grievance-handling and Activities for further details).

Managers should not, however, assume that 'offending' employees are fully conversant with the contents and operation of the organisation's employment policies. It is often the case that our working lives are so busy that we are forced to adopt a 'need to know' approach regarding the information that we take in. Thus previously exemplary employees would have had no need to know intimately the workings of the disciplinary procedure.

So what can the employer do to bring the disciplinary rules and procedures to the attention of the workforce? There are several options – incorporate this subject into the induction programme, make copies readily available to all employees, provide training for newly appointed line managers and refresher training for existing ones (organisations often wait for disasters to occur before doing this, eg a finding of unfair dismissal at a tribunal hearing!). Further, if management decide to 'clamp down' on certain activities, eg time-keeping, 'casual' sickness absence (see Figure 4 opposite), or private work during company time, they should publicise this by, say, including it on the agenda of team meetings, by issuing memoranda, and by compiling reports highlighting statistical trends.

We have now looked at the content and operation of disciplinary rules and procedures as well as the effect of relevant employment legislation. Before moving on to the issue of grievance-handling, we need to consider whether disciplinary action will be necessary. The check-list in Figure 4, adapted from Croner's *Personnel assistant's handbook* (p9–8) should help.

GRIEVANCE-HANDLING

Unlike the case with discipline, there is little detailed guidance provided by bodies such as ACAS regarding good practice in handling grievances in the workplace. Generally, however, it is accepted that employees must be provided with a means by which they can officially raise complaints and seek redress. In your role as personnel practitioner, you should encourage this process so that problems can be dealt with at an early stage before they start to affect other employees. Otherwise they may escalate into more serious issues and can even result in industrial action. This is more likely if the grievance raised affects a large number of employees rather than just a handful. Nevertheless, it is difficult to predict which unresolved grievances could provide the trigger for industrial unrest, eg a poorly handled redundancy selection programme affecting only one or two employees could have a disruptive effect on the motivation and productivity of the rest of the workforce. In theory, then, managers should welcome grievances, but the experience of many employees is that management view those who raise them as nuisances or troublemakers. What is your view?

As has already been stated, ERA states that details of the grievance procedure must be contained in the written statement of employment. The statement must include details of 'the name or description of the person with whom the employee can raise a grievance and the manner in which such applications can be made' and an explanation of any additional steps in the grievance procedure. This requirement is applicable to all organisations, regardless of their size.

Thus you should ensure that employees are aware of the existence of the grievance procedure by publicising it through the induction programme for new employees, making copies readily available to all employees, making known the results of successfully resolved grievances, and by providing specialist training for all levels of management likely to be involved in handling grievances. It cannot be stressed enough how important it is for grievances to be dealt with in an appropriate manner. If an employee has decided to make a complaint formal it usually means that he or she feels strongly about the issue and will not, therefore, appreciate a manager attempting to trivialise the complaint. Further, if employees

Figure 4 Disciplinary action check-list

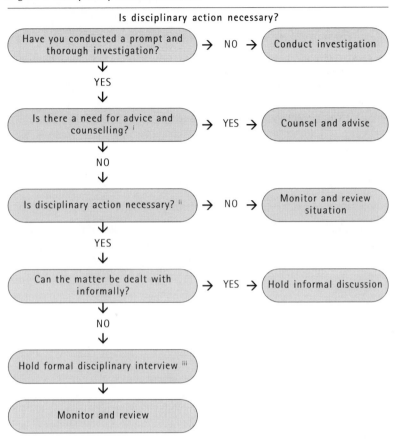

Is disciplinary action necessary?

Have you conducted a prompt and thorough investigation? → NO → Conduct investigation

↓ YES ↓

Is there a need for advice and counselling? [i] → YES → Counsel and advise

↓ NO ↓

Is disciplinary action necessary? [ii] → NO → Monitor and review situation

↓ YES ↓

Can the matter be dealt with informally? → YES → Hold informal discussion

↓ NO ↓

Hold formal disciplinary interview [iii]

↓

Monitor and review

Footnotes

i We have already mentioned that managers may rightly decide that, though a breach of the disciplinary rules has occurred, there are extenuating circumstances which merit consideration and render disciplinary action unwise or unjustifiable. The manager may decide that counselling is a more appropriate option and either personally undertake this role or arrange for a 'specialist' to do so (see Chapter 9 for more information on this).

ii Case-law dictates that disciplinary procedures are inappropriate in most circumstances relating to sickness absence whether it is a) long term or b) short term as follows:

   a) You should follow a separate procedure covering informing and maintaining frequent contacts with the employee, gathering medical evidence, and considering alternative employment before any decision to dismiss (or retire) the employee (see the ACAS Advisory Handbook: *Discipline at work* for further information). You should also bear in mind the provisions of the Disability Discrimination Act 1995 before taking your final decision (see Chapter 3 for further details).

   b) If investigations show that absences are not genuine (for instance, an employee returning from a period of absence with a deep sun tan might lead you to investigate more fully!) then you should follow the normal disciplinary procedure as this is a conduct issue. However, it is often the case that suspected 'casual' absences cannot be proven and then you should be wary of treating absences as misconduct. Do not despair though as unacceptable levels of attendance can be dealt with by ensuring a fair review of the attendance record, allowing the employee to make representations, gathering medical evidence, seeking to help the employee to improve their attendance record and warning them of the consequences should this not occur. If there is no adequate improvement then dismissal will be justifiable (see IDS Brief: Employment Law Supplement No 54: Sickness and Disability for further information).

iii See the section below on the Disciplinary Interview.

perceive that management never seem to respond to formal complaints, then the incidence of grievances may fall; this does not then mean that there are no problems but that employees are too demotivated to raise them. This is unlikely to result in a healthy and stable working situation.

Examples of issues likely to be raised under the grievance procedure within most organisations, large or small, are as follows:

- working conditions eg light, heat
- use of equipment eg poorly maintained
- personality clashes
- refused requests eg annual leave, shift changes
- shortfalls in pay eg late bonus payments, adjustments to overtime pay
- allocation of 'perks' eg Sunday overtime working.

The type of issues likely to be raised as grievances varies from one workplace to the next. Unlike more sophisticated or larger organisations, small establishments may have only a grievance procedure and will not have in place other consultation arrangements or appeals mechanisms to deal with complaints about:

- disciplinary action
- safety issues
- job evaluation results
- sickness absence dismissals
- catering matters
- discrimination or harassment claims
- negotiated pay deals
- terms and conditions.

You should be prepared to advise employees as to the most suitable procedure to use to raise a grievance.

The last two examples on the list above are collective rather than individual issues and are likely to be dealt with, in a unionised environment, under the organisation's disputes procedure (see the next section). In non-unionised environments, individuals may be invited to 'negotiate' their pay and terms and conditions on an individual basis, but in reality the balance of power is very much on the side of the employer, so individuals may have a limited influence only.

We shall now look more specifically at the content of grievance procedures.

Grievance procedures

Grievance procedures are the means by which employees can formally raise complaints with management. The aim is to resolve these issues as near as possible to the location of the original complaint. The following principles apply to grievance procedures. They should be:

- equitable in the way in which employees are treated

- simple to understand

- rapid in their application.

A successful outcome of a grievance would be a solution that satisfies all the parties. For example, an employee with a justifiable complaint about the unequal distribution of overtime would probably be satisfied if a new written procedure was drawn up to avoid this in the future. Management are also likely to be happy, because this should minimise the likelihood of similar complaints in the future. Sometimes, though, there is no satisfactory solution available, so management's job becomes one not of problem-solving but of explanation and persuasion. Employees will often initially view the effect of a decision as unfair but will be more likely to accept it if they know why it was made.

There are no absolute rules regarding the content of grievance procedures, but generally they follow the stages set out below:

Informal stage   The employee should first raise the matter with his or her immediate supervisor.

Stage 1   If the matter remains unresolved, the employee can raise the matter formally, via a representative if he or she wishes, with the immediate supervisor.

Stage 2   If the matter remains unresolved, a meeting will be arranged with the employee, the representative (if applicable), and the departmental manager.

Stage 3   If the matter remains unresolved, a meeting will be arranged to include the functional director and the union regional officer (if applicable).

NB Each stage will be timebound in order that a speedy resolution can be sought.

If there is a failure to agree at Stage 3, the arrangements outlined in the organisation's disputes procedure come into play eg independent conciliation or arbitration or, possibly, a ballot for industrial action. Thus the grievance procedure and the disputes procedure dovetail at the final stage. Any form of industrial action is precluded until all the stages have been completed and a failure to agree recorded ie the procedure has been exhausted.

An example of a grievance might be that of a female employee who has been nominated to attend a weekend training event. The employee does not want to go and approaches her immediate supervisor to complain that she was only given two weeks' notice and will find it difficult to arrange for childcare. Any supervisor faced with this problem will find it difficult to reach a decision that is satisfactory to all parties. On the assumption that the training is necessary and will be expensive to cancel, the supervisor will have to investigate the following before reaching a decision:

- Does the contract of employment contain a clause referring to 'out of hours' training?

- What has happened in the past in similar circumstances (ie custom and practice)?

- Has the employee been willing to attend training events in the past?

- What is known about the employee's domestic circumstances?

- Can alternative arrangements be made to accommodate this training?

If the employee is not satisfied by the response she receives at this informal stage, she may decide to pursue her grievance more formally by invoking Stage 1 of the grievance procedure.

Personnel practitioners often feel that they are in a difficult position in handling grievances. Generally, their only formalised role is to take receipt of grievances at Stage 1 and onwards. A good record-keeping system should assist them in determining whether any previous decisions have established precedents for handling similar grievances. More proactive personnel practitioners will initiate the investigations and discussions necessary in order to address grievances and may also attend grievance hearings. These actions will help them to keep a tight rein on such matters so that line managers do not seek resolutions to grievances without thinking through the consequences for the rest of the organisation. For instance, in our previous example regarding the unequal distribution of overtime, it is unlikely that changes to overtime allocation arrangements within one department could be taken in isolation of all other departments. Dependent on the organisational position of the personnel department (and personal standing of its members), personnel practitioners will have varying degrees of success in seeking to influence such decisions.

We shall now examine the role of personnel practitioners in discipline and grievance-handling in the workplace.

THE ROLE OF PERSONNEL PRACTITIONERS

In the above text we have tended to concentrate on the role of supervisors and line managers in implementing the rules and procedures applicable to discipline and grievance-handling. As personnel practitioners, you will obviously adopt the same role when dealing with your own staff but are also likely to carry out the following roles, depending on the detail of your organisation's rules and procedures:

An advisory role to line managers
In this capacity your advice is sought before disciplinary action is taken or grievances are addressed. This will help to ensure a consistency of approach across the organisation as, in this role, you need to be familiar with relevant employment legislation, case-law, and accepted good practice. You should also have an appreciation of how such situations have been dealt with in the past and the likely repercussions of decisions taken for the future, as well as being the 'authority' regarding the operation and interpretation of your own rules and procedures. (It has already been stressed that industrial action could result from poorly managed disciplinary and grievance situations – most managers would agree that troubleshooting is generally preferable to firefighting!)

An overseeing role
In this you bring possible disciplinary infringements to the attention of line managers for their action, eg following a periodic check on attendance records and/or sickness notification and certification records. This again

serves to ensure a standardised approach to organisation-wide problems but difficulties may be experienced when line managers use this as an opportunity to abdicate responsibility back to the personnel department.

A secretarial role

You carry out this in the disciplinary and grievance hearings themselves to ensure that detailed and accurate records are kept. This is especially necessary in the event of appeals against disciplinary action or unresolved grievances that are progressing to the next stage and (every personnel practitioners' nightmare) industrial tribunal hearings. See the Appendix to Chapter 6 for a check-list for taking notes of disciplinary interviews (this check-list could also, with some slight adaptation, be used for grievance interviews).

A decision-making role

This regards the action that should be taken in a disciplinary situation or the means to (hopefully) satisfactorily conclude a grievance application. The authority for this role must be stated in the appropriate procedures (except where, as a personnel practitioner, you are acting as the line manager for your own staff). This role is more likely to be adopted in a smaller organisation where, for instance, the personnel manager has the authority only to dismiss, thus reserving the independence of a third party of higher status, the managing director, to hear any appeals.

A training or educational role

This is to ensure that managers follow the procedure correctly and are trained to carry out interviews. Training may be formal or informal, as appropriate. Most managers, unlike personnel practitioners, do not have a wide experience of handling disciplinaries or grievances; they may have undergone formal training some time previously but need some coaching to give them the confidence to lead an interview.

Please note that it is essential that the identification of the 'hat' (or 'hats') being worn by the personnel practitioner in disciplinary matters and grievance-handling is absolutely clear. Industrial tribunal cases regarding unfair dismissal claims have been lost by employers when it became apparent that the decision to dismiss was taken by someone other than the person named in the procedure as having sufficient authority.

The next section will deal with the skills necessary for successful disciplinary and grievance interviews.

INTERVIEWING SKILLS

We have seen that personnel practitioners (and line managers) need to acquire a great deal of knowledge in order to be competent in handling disciplinary and grievance situations. They also need certain skills – written and oral communications, investigatory skills, persuasion, judgement, decision-making, analytical reasoning, to name but a few. At no time is the need for this knowledge and these skills more evident than when carrying out the disciplinary or grievance interview, and we shall now examine accepted good practice.

Thorough preparation will help to ensure that interviewers are as professional as possible, regardless of their level of experience. It can safely be said that few managers actually relish the idea of conducting a disciplinary interview and, as has already been suggested, are more likely to view grievance-handling as an unpleasant chore rather than a rewarding experience (a visit to the dentist might engender only slightly less enthusiasm!).

Many of the skills required to carry out satisfactory selection interviews (see Chapter 4) are equally applicable to disciplinary and grievance interviewing, eg:

- preparing for the interview

- preparing the environment

- using open and probing questions

- active listening

- maintaining good eye contact

- using appropriate body language

- using silence

- keeping control of the subject matter and timing

- taking notes

- remaining unemotional

- providing clarification

- summarising.

There are obviously differences in the purposes of the three types of interviews: selection, disciplinary, and grievance. Thus it is good practice, in selection interviews, to establish a rapport with the interviewee; this generally involves a warm welcome and friendly exchange in an attempt to relax the interviewee so that he or she can perform at his or her optimum during the interview. This behaviour is obviously not entirely appropriate in a disciplinary interview and also, to some extent, a grievance interview. If you are too familiar or too personal there is a danger of not being taken seriously, or of possibly being drawn into arguments and straying into personality issues. A lack of perceived seriousness could invalidate a disciplinary warning or lead employees with a grievance to the conclusion that their views are unimportant. Conversely, an overly formal and impersonal style may seem to compromise reasonableness. Implementation of procedures in ways that are devoid of humanity is likely to lead to dissatisfaction and, in the case of dismissals, successful industrial tribunal claims. You need to strike a balance between the two approaches.

In summary, the key points applicable to both disciplinary and grievance interviews are to:

- stay calm and in control

- be reasonable and objective

- be factual and unemotional.

You should find the following charts (Figures 5 and 6 on pages 101–2) useful 'step-by-step' approaches.

Figure 5 The disciplinary interview

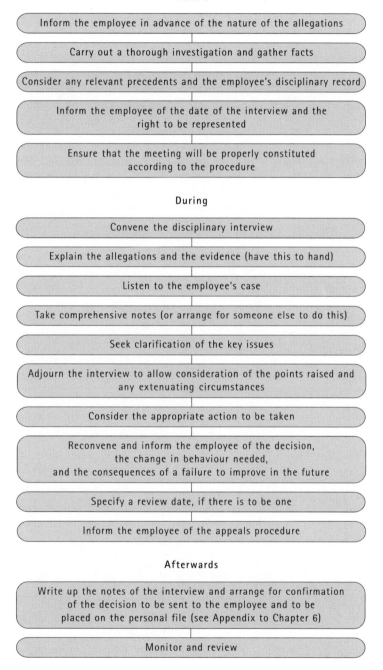

Before

Inform the employee in advance of the nature of the allegations

Carry out a thorough investigation and gather facts

Consider any relevant precedents and the employee's disciplinary record

Inform the employee of the date of the interview and the right to be represented

Ensure that the meeting will be properly constituted according to the procedure

During

Convene the disciplinary interview

Explain the allegations and the evidence (have this to hand)

Listen to the employee's case

Take comprehensive notes (or arrange for someone else to do this)

Seek clarification of the key issues

Adjourn the interview to allow consideration of the points raised and any extenuating circumstances

Consider the appropriate action to be taken

Reconvene and inform the employee of the decision, the change in behaviour needed, and the consequences of a failure to improve in the future

Specify a review date, if there is to be one

Inform the employee of the appeals procedure

Afterwards

Write up the notes of the interview and arrange for confirmation of the decision to be sent to the employee and to be placed on the personal file (see Appendix to Chapter 6)

Monitor and review

NB Halt the proceedings at any point where it is apparent that the use of the disciplinary procedure is inappropriate.

Figure 6 The grievance interview (formal stages)

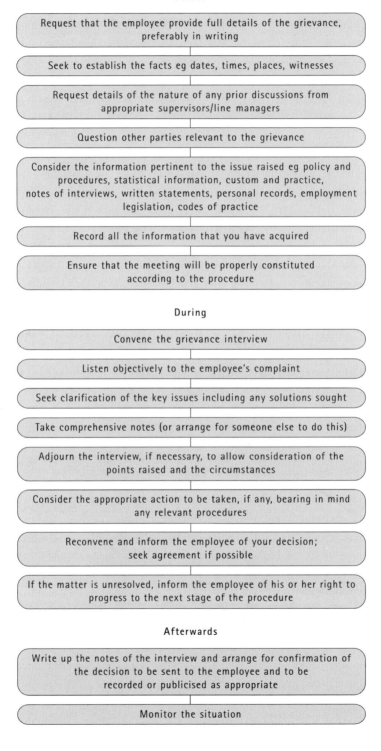

Before

Request that the employee provide full details of the grievance, preferably in writing

Seek to establish the facts eg dates, times, places, witnesses

Request details of the nature of any prior discussions from appropriate supervisors/line managers

Question other parties relevant to the grievance

Consider the information pertinent to the issue raised eg policy and procedures, statistical information, custom and practice, notes of interviews, written statements, personal records, employment legislation, codes of practice

Record all the information that you have acquired

Ensure that the meeting will be properly constituted according to the procedure

During

Convene the grievance interview

Listen objectively to the employee's complaint

Seek clarification of the key issues including any solutions sought

Take comprehensive notes (or arrange for someone else to do this)

Adjourn the interview, if necessary, to allow consideration of the points raised and the circumstances

Consider the appropriate action to be taken, if any, bearing in mind any relevant procedures

Reconvene and inform the employee of your decision; seek agreement if possible

If the matter is unresolved, inform the employee of his or her right to progress to the next stage of the procedure

Afterwards

Write up the notes of the interview and arrange for confirmation of the decision to be sent to the employee and to be recorded or publicised as appropriate

Monitor the situation

SUMMARY

You should now be familiar with the 'theory' and practice of discipline and grievance-handling. We have looked at the content and operation of disciplinary rules and disciplinary and grievance procedures, as well as their importance, relevant legislation, and accepted good practice. The knowledge and skills necessary for dealing with these issues have also been examined, specifically with regard to the role(s) played by personnel practitioners.

In order to reinforce this learning you are now advised to attempt at least one or two of the Activities listed below. Finally, a list of references, legislative Acts, suggested further reading, and recommended video titles is provided at the end of this chapter.

ACTIVITIES

1 Familiarise yourself with the written particulars of employment issued to new employees (and to existing employees on request) within your organisation. Does the statement include the following details?

   • any disciplinary rules applicable

   • the name or description of the person to whom an employee can apply if dissatisfied with a disciplinary decision, and the manner in which such applications can be made

   • the name or description of the person with whom the employee can raise a grievance and the manner in which such applications should be made

   • an explanation of any additional steps in the disciplinary or grievance procedures.

   If there are any omissions, bring them to the attention of the person(s) responsible for issuing written particulars of employment.

2 Regarding the issue of publicising rules and procedures applicable to disciplinary and grievance situations, write down six specific ways in which employees could become better informed in your organisation. Discuss these with one or more of your learning sources.

3 If you are inexperienced in handling disciplinaries, ask if you could sit in on a disciplinary interview as an observer only. Try to identify good and bad practices (diplomatically, of course). Did you agree with the decision reached? If not, seek to discuss the reasons for the decision with the manager concerned.

4 If you are inexperienced in handling grievances, ask to be given details of a recently submitted grievance. Peruse all the information available and ask appropriate questions of any managers involved, if possible. When you have as much information available as possible, answer the following question: did you agree with the decision reached? If not, seek to discuss the reasons for the decision with the manager concerned.

APPENDIX TO CHAPTER 6

Check-list for taking notes of disciplinary interviews
The following check-list should assist you in ensuring that your written notes fully meet the need to:

• provide sufficient information to whoever is responsible for issuing the confirmation letter to the employee (if this is necessary)

• provide a useful justification and record of the action taken at this stage should the situation deteriorate further (possibly resulting in an unfair dismissal claim being heard at an industrial tribunal).

Do the notes include:

YES/NO

1 the date, venue, and start-time of the interview

2 an account of those attending the interview and their roles

3 details of the allegations stated to the employee

4 details of the employee's response

5 a record of any adjournments and approximate timings

6 consideration of the employee's previous record

7 the decision on whether disciplinary action was appropriate or not and the type of action taken with the appropriate time-scale

8 a clear statement of intent if improvement does not occur

9 reference to the right to appeal and the finish time of the interview

10 reference to its author plus a date and signature?

REFERENCES AND FURTHER READING

The following are available from the Advisory, Conciliation and Arbitration Service (ACAS), ACAS Reader Ltd, P.O. Box 16, Earl Shilton, Leicester, LE9 8ZZ; tel. 01455 852 225:

Advisory booklet on absence. (Undated) Leicester, ACAS.

Advisory handbook on discipline at work. (amended 1989) Leicester, ACAS.

Advisory booklet on employment policies. (Undated) Leicester, ACAS.

The following are available from Croner Publications Ltd, Croner House, London Road, Kingston-upon-Thames, Surrey, KT2 6SR; tel. 0181 547 3465:

Croner's employment law. Kingston-upon-Thames, Croner Publications.

Croner's personnel assistant's handbook. Kingston-upon-Thames, Croner Publications.

Croner's reference book for employers. Kingston-upon-Thames, Croner Publications.

The following are available from the Institute of Personnel and Development (IPD), IPD House, Camp Road, London, SW19 4UX; tel. 0181 263 3387:

FOWLER A. (1996) *The disciplinary interview*. London, Institute of Personnel and Development.

JAMES P. and LEWIS D. (1992) *Discipline*. London, Institute of Personnel and Development.

The following is available from Incomes Data Services (IDS), 193 St John Street, London, EC1V 4LS; tel. 0171 250 3434:

IDS brief: employment law supplement no 54: sickness & disability. November 1988.

ACTS OF PARLIAMENT/CODES OF PRACTICE

Code of practice 1: disciplinary practice and procedures in employment. (1977) Leicester, ACAS.

Disability Discrimination Act 1995

Employment Rights Act 1996

VIDEOS

I'd like a word with you. (1996) Video Arts (on disciplinary handling).

No smoke without fire. (1986) Melrose (on disciplinary and grievance handling).

Unfair dismissal. (1985) Video Arts.

7 Performance management

INTRODUCTION

In an article published in *Personnel Management* magazine (the predecessor to *People Management*) in late 1991, Stephen Bevan and Marc Thompson reported on their major survey into the operation of performance management within a range of organisations. They questioned personnel managers in order to find out whether they had heard of the term 'performance management' and, if they had, what it meant to them. Not surprisingly, the majority claimed to have heard of performance management, but their views on its purpose and what it involved varied enormously. (See Bevan and Thompson (1991).)

At around the same time, the Institute of Manpower Studies (IMS) was commissioned by the Institute of Personnel Management (now the Institute of Personnel and Development) to carry out a survey of performance management in 1,800 organisations. Less than 20 per cent of responding organisations claimed to operate performance management systems. Of those that did, there were similarities in their approaches to managing employee performance but there was little consistency in their definitions of performance management.

The picture today is very similar, in that many organisations claim to adopt performance management techniques, of which there are several, but the mix of these activities varies greatly from one organisation to the next.

In the next section, we shall consider why performance management is important for personnel practitioners and the organisations they work for before looking at the differences between performance appraisal and performance management. We shall then go on to look at performance appraisal in more detail: its purposes, history, and trends, and the various components of schemes, including the issue of objective-setting, as well as the benefits and best practice considerations. Sections on payment systems, particularly performance-related pay (PRP), and the legal considerations follow. Finally, we shall pay attention to the differing roles played by the personnel practitioner and the skills necessary for effective interviewing.

Before doing this we would draw your attention to another distinction in terms: performance management *v* managing performance. The first term tends to be used in reference to activities designed to motivate and encourage employees to work towards objectives that are in line with organisational goals. The second term includes managing good and poor performance, and therefore encompasses activities such as disciplinary procedures and absence control. We shall be concentrating here on performance management, not managing performance, and would refer you to the chapter on disciplinary and grievance-handling (Chapter 6) for reference to managing poor performers via the disciplinary route. Please note that the two processes of disciplinary procedures and performance appraisal should complement each other in these circumstances.

WHY IS IT IMPORTANT?

Suffice it to say here that, without performance management, work will not be organised to achieve the optimum results. For instance:

- Salespeople may be achieving their sales targets, but the discounts and special incentives that they offer customers in order to do so have a detrimental effect on the profit margins – profit being the driving force of the company they are working for.

- A university lecturer whose brief is to recruit a certain number of students to a full-time course of study may find that, in the current economic climate, there is less money available for grants and other means of finance. Thus there is a smaller pool of potential candidates with the requisite qualifications than in previous years. The college tutor decides that, rather than failing to reach the target, he or she will have to lower the entry requirements to the course. This will satisfy the immediate 'input' need but is likely to lead to problems at the 'output' stage, because a larger percentage of students may fail to get the qualification under study. The university's finances (and business goals) will be dependent on the overall input *and* output targets being reached.

- Computer helpline staff may point to the numbers of users they have helped over a period of time as an indication of their hard work and efficiency. However, this figure does not take account of those users who failed to get through the busy switchboard system and had to seek assistance elsewhere. If the main aims of the computer company are to increase market share and maintain customer loyalty, then this aspect of 'after sales' service would need to be re-evaluated. The dissatisfied group of customers will be less inclined to buy from the same supplier again and will also not recommend friends and colleagues to do so.

Thus we can see, in the above examples, that the employees concerned were all seeking to do what they had been told to do ie they were probably being efficient, but were they being effective?

Efficient – doing things right

Effective – doing the right things

The answer is no: in each case, insufficient thought had been giving to ensuring that employees' individual targets were geared towards the overall business goals. The key is to ensure that there is a clear link between the tasks and activities that employees are involved in and the achievement of organisational goals. It is also crucial that evaluation methods are set up to judge whether this is the case. We shall return to this question in the following section.

PERFORMANCE APPRAISAL v PERFORMANCE MANAGEMENT

In very simple terms, performance appraisal is the 'tail that wags the dog' in its relationship with performance management. The exercise of appraising performance is necessarily retrospective, because it concerns making a judgement about the past performance of employees. Appraisals can be used to improve current performance by providing feedback on strengths and weaknesses. (NB 'Weaknesses' are probably better labelled 'areas for improvement' if we wish to emphasise the positive and constructive nature of this feedback.) Appraisals can, therefore, be effective in increasing employee motivation and, ultimately, organisational performance. Performance appraisal can, and should, be linked to a performance-improvement process, and can then also be used to identify training needs and potential, agree future objectives, focus on career development, and solve problems. One such performance improvement process would be a performance management system (PMS).

Performance management is a vehicle for the continuous improvement of business performance via a co-ordinated programme of people management *interventions* (or systems). Mike Walters (1995: *x*) lists these interventions as follows:

- strategic planning

- the definition of organisational goals, priorities, and values

- the identification and application of appropriate performance goals and measures for the organisation, for key processes, for functions, and for individual employees

- appraisal

- personal development planning

- learning and development activities

- various forms of PRP.

The last of these, PRP, demonstrates the need to ensure a link between the PMS and your organisation's payment system and administration. As we point out in Chapter 8, good computer links between the payroll and other personnel systems are often difficult to make. If, for instance, poor communications (or links) lead to late or incorrect payment of PRP, this will be detrimental to the motivational effects of a good PMS. Each and every intervention needs to be clearly linked together in order that their overall impact on business performance can be carefully co-ordinated. We discuss payment systems and PRP in particular in more detail in a later section.

As we have already stated, there is no universally accepted definition of performance management, but we can safely say that it is a much broader concept than performance appraisal. To demonstrate this, consider the example of a small owner-managed garage. The company sells and hires cars as well as running a shop to sell petrol and other goods. Several staff are employed, each specialising in one of the above areas or in accounting or clerical positions. The majority of staff enjoy their jobs and feel that they are reasonably well rewarded in terms of financial and other benefits.

There is no formal means of appraising staff, but the owner-manager does see all staff on a regular basis to inform them of their progress and to discuss any problems. He adopts a well used 'open-door' policy. In the main, the employees are highly motivated and industrious, and achieve high efficiencies in the work that they do.

With such a favourable environment, you might assume that the overall business performance of the company would be optimised. You would however be wrong, as the owner-manager has recently been shocked to discover that the profits for the last tax year were not as high as he had expected. To cut a long story short, he employed a placement student studying a personnel management qualification to investigate the reasons for this enigma. The answer, when it was discovered, was a simple one: the employees were hard-working but, because there was no link between their personal objectives and the organisational goal (in this case, profit), the result was that, though they could be deemed to be efficient, they were not effective.

After a period of research, which was mostly comprised of interviews with staff, the student produced a comprehensive report for the owner-manager. This covered her research findings as well as providing a lot of information on performance management in general. The owner-manager saw that there were some systems already in place but that there was a lack of co-ordination between them all. For instance, the car sales staff were expected to provide relief cover when the person employed on the hire car counter was at lunch. This was resented by the sales staff because they felt that they might miss sales opportunities owing to being 'tied up' at the car hire desk. Their individual and team performance sales targets were naturally seen as a much higher priority than the need to provide a quality service to potential car hire customers. Further, the former activities were rewarded by the payment of commissions, whereas the latter 'customer care' activities were not formally assessed by their manager and did not attract any sort of reward, financial or otherwise. The hiring of cars, however, did contribute substantially to the overall profit level of the company and, unlike car sales, provided a steadier flow of income, because car hire is less subject to seasonal trends. To the owner-manager, who set the business goals, it was equally important to maintain a good reputation for selling quality cars as it was to provide a reliable and competitive car hire service.

With the help of the student, the owner-manager decided to clarify the business strategy, review the existing interventions, and to scrap, modify, or replace them (as appropriate) in line with the company's goals. However, he also learnt that a balance needs to be struck between reward-driven and development-driven approaches. This is because performance management systems can fail when their implementation becomes dominated by the link to reward. Thus schemes designed to improve employee performance, eg incentive, bonus, profit-sharing, and commission approaches, can have the opposite effect when employee expectations are not realised. In fact, the owner-manager had experienced this in the past when there was an unexpected rise in the price of petrol. In order to preserve his profits, he was forced to reduce the pot of money available for a discretionary bonus paid to the shop staff. They therefore received much less than had been anticipated based on their past experiences. Although the reasons were fully explained at the time, it took quite a while for the shop staff to regain their normal levels of motivation: they felt that, though they had been working hard, they had been punished for something that was outside their control.

The main lesson that the owner-manager learnt was that there should be clear and co-ordinated two-way links in all the stages between the strategic plan and individual objectives (see Figure 7).

Figure 7 The two-way links model

This does not mean that individuals cannot seek to satisfy their own personal objectives, but it does help to focus them on their own roles and contribution to the overall business performance. The result will hopefully be a motivational one as their efforts are directed at those activities which best serve organisational goals. (Further consideration of this motivational aspect is provided in the following text.)

The issues are the same regardless of the size of organisation; the key is to ensure that there are feedback mechanisms in place, as demonstrated in Figure 7. To return to our example, the owner-manager was able with the help of the student to begin the process of ensuring that the new and revamped PMS was fully co-ordinated and geared towards the achievement of business objectives. This was not a trouble-free process, but the result was an encouraging improvement in the level of profits in the following year. One example of a new intervention was the one set up to reward the achievement of a monthly car hire target, based on maximising the use of the hire cars. The car hire employee was sent on a selling course in order to improve her skills at getting new business (she had previously viewed her job as simply an administrative one). The system involved accumulating points towards the team target and included all those staff who provided cover on the car hire desk. This may not have been a perfect solution but did ensure that all the staff involved were 'rowing in the same direction'.

We shall now consider one aspect within the wider framework of performance management: performance appraisal. There have been major developments in the field of performance appraisal in recent years and, after explaining its purposes, we shall briefly cover its history and trends.

PERFORMANCE APPRAISAL

Purposes

There are three main groups of purposes for performance appraisal (and most schemes incorporate at least two of these):

- *performance reviews* – managers discuss with employees progress in their current posts, their strengths, and the areas requiring further development, in order to improve *current performance*

- *potential reviews* – managers discuss with employees the opportunities for progression, and the type of work they will be fitted for in the future and how this can be achieved, by identifying their *developmental needs*

- *reward reviews* – these are usually separate from the appraisal system but the decisions on *rewards* such as pay, benefits, promotion, and self-fulfilment are fed by the information provided by performance appraisal.

Properly conducted performance appraisal interviews will usually involve a manager and employee in a constructive discussion concerning the employee's recent performance (say, over the previous 12 months), plans for improved performance, and plans for meeting the developmental needs of the employee. At a later stage, a reward review interview will be arranged so that the manager and employee can openly discuss, for instance, the level of PRP that has been awarded.

As personnel practitioners, you are likely to know already that such events do not always go according to plan. For instance:

- Not all employees are good performers, and managers may not be as constructive as they should in their delivery of feedback.

- In an organisation in which there are few promotion opportunities, employees (and their managers) may view learning and development activities as somewhat pointless.

- If a high-performing individual's expectation of PRP is not realised (often through factors outside their own control) then he or she may decide not to try so hard to achieve targets or objectives in the future.

Thus the motivational effect of performance appraisal is often debatable. On a positive note, Hale and Whitlam (1995: 2) provide an interesting model – see Table 7 on page 112 – of how performance appraisal can be used to satisfy employees' basic motivational needs (based on the now famous research of Peters and Waterman (1982) into successful organisations).

We shall discuss the skills of performance appraisal interviewing, applicable in both good and poor performer situations, in a later section.

History and trends

As we have already said, with the emergence of performance management the main change in performance appraisal schemes has been the establishment of clearer links between individual objectives and

Table 7 Performance appraisal and employee motivation

Peters and Waterman factors	How performance appraisal can satisfy these needs
Need for meaning	Clear linking of individual jobs with the objectives of the organisation
Need for control	Joint discussion between subordinate and manager regarding future job priorities and targets
Need for positive reinforcement	Provision of effective feedback from manager to subordinate
Actions shape attitudes and beliefs	Performance appraisal as the starting-point for deciding future action, which entails senior-level commitment to help the individual develop

organisational goals. In recent years there have been other changes, many of which have complemented this principle. Hale and Whitlam (1995: 19–22) provide the following breakdown of recent tends.

From traits to results-based assessment
In the 1960s a Management by Objectives (MbO) approach evolved, based on a more scientific approach and on more forward-focused performance appraisal. Thus there was a move from schemes that made judgements on employees' traits and behaviours such as leadership, teamwork, and diligence to those where the emphasis was placed on the achievement of results and outputs linked to targets. MbO schemes are still in existence today, but many have foundered because they failed to establish the link between individual and organisational objectives.

From effort to results focus
In line with the MbO approach, the method of assessment has shifted away from effort measures such as concentration, enthusiasm, and self-organisation to results measures such as quality of work, sound decision-making, and financial performance.

From judgmental to joint problem-solving
The closed type of appraisal scheme in which the manager told the employee what judgement had been made on his or her performance has given way to a more open, joint identification of strengths and weaknesses, as well as joint planning for improved future performance. (In line with this we have seen self-appraisal play a much more important role in the whole process – indeed it may form the basis for the appraisal interview in some schemes.)

From managerial to all jobs
Whereas many organisations still operate separate schemes for appraising managerial and non-managerial posts, there has been a move towards incorporating employees at all levels within the performance appraisal system.

We can add a further trend to this list:

From top-down to 360-degree appraisals
Appraisals have moved on from a fairly simple manager–subordinate (or top-down) relationship (possibly including self-appraisal) to 360-degree appraisals, involving stakeholders who provide feedback on an individual's performance.

Figure 8 Stakeholders in 360-degree appraisal

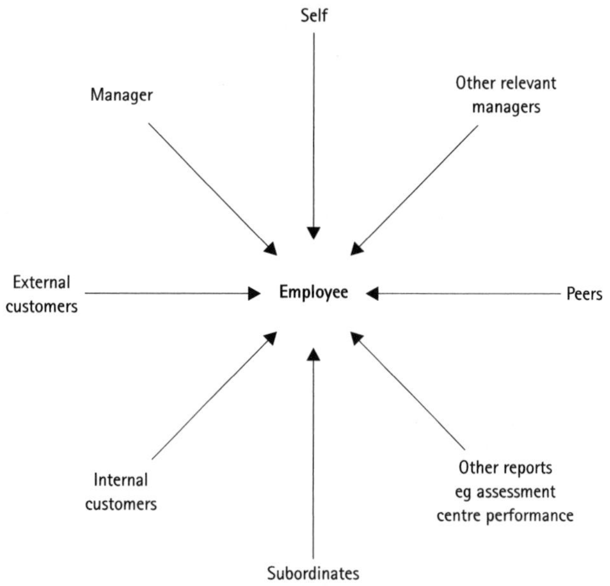

Self

Manager

Other relevant
managers

External
customers

Employee

Peers

Internal
customers

Other reports
eg assessment
centre performance

Subordinates

Figure 8 shows an example of the stakeholders that might be involved in an individual's appraisal. There is a great variety in the way in which 360-degree appraisal is implemented in organisations. On the one hand, the appraisal interview may include all the stakeholders giving face-to-face feedback to the appraisee (who may well feel that the term 'victim' is more appropriate here!). On the other hand, some organisations operate systems whereby the collection of feedback from the chosen stakeholders is done via formally constructed questionnaires. This information is then collated and fed back to the individual by a neutral third party (possibly a personnel practitioner). Larger organisations have even invested in computer packages to cut down on the administrative burden attached to collecting and collating this information on a large scale.

As a result of the above trends, most performance appraisal schemes nowadays follow the stages of the performance review cycle as set out in Figure 9.

Figure 9 The performance review cycle

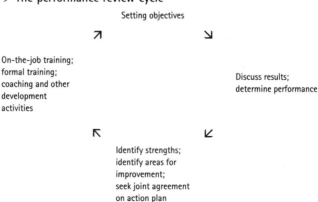

Setting objectives

On-the-job training;
formal training;
coaching and other
development
activities

Discuss results;
determine performance

Identify strengths;
identify areas for
improvement;
seek joint agreement
on action plan

We shall discuss the much-debated issue of objective-setting shortly, but first let's look at the various components of performance appraisal schemes.

Components of performance appraisal schemes

If you are designing a performance appraisal scheme, you need first to determine its purpose (or purposes) and seek to integrate the new scheme into your PMS, if one exists. Against this backdrop you then need to make the following decisions, depending on the organisational circumstances:

- Who is to be appraised? That is, you must decide what levels or functions of employees are to be involved.

- Who appraises? This could be the employee; the manager only; the manager and subordinates; or other stakeholders (see the previous section regarding 360-degree appraisal).

- What is to be appraised, and what criteria will be used? The options include traits *v* results, and achievement of objectives.

- What assessment methods will you employ? You could opt for a descriptive or narrative report; a check-list; ratings or gradings; comparison with objectives; comparison with others (ranking individuals in order of performance); critical incidents (recorded incidents of positive and negative behaviours); or competence-based (assessment against the achievement of set standards).

- Will you incorporate assessment of promotion potential; a link to reward or a salary review; a means of appeal against a (perceived) unfair assessment?

- How often is the formal appraisal interview to be carried out – once every three, six, or twelve months? Will you include interim reviews to accommodate the pace of change?

- How will you ensure that the action points are implemented (eg the meeting of training needs)?

- How will you evaluate success (ie the achievement of the purpose(s) of the scheme)?

The ACAS Advisory Booklet No 11, *Employee appraisal*, lists the following key points for successful appraisal schemes:

- Make sure that senior managers are fully committed to the idea of appraisals.

- Consult with managers, employees, and trade union representatives about the design and implementation of appraisals before they are introduced.

- Monitor schemes regularly.

- Give appraisers adequate training to enable them to make fair and objective assessments and to carry out effective appraisal interviews

- Keep the scheme as simple and straightforward as possible.

We could add the following suggestions:

- Before implementing the scheme across the whole organisation, carry out a pilot run in, say, one department in order to gain invaluable feedback on possible teething problems which can then be solved before the main launch. Start with the most senior people in your pilot area, so that you gain their commitment and encourage them to lead by example and to cascade their learning downwards.

• Ensure that appraisers and appraisees jointly identify strengths and areas for improvement, and that appraisers provide constructive feedback on performance and support the appraisee in meeting their development needs in line with business goals.

We have mentioned the place of objective-setting several times within the context of performance appraisal and performance management. We shall now seek to examine this concept further.

Objective-setting
The recent trend from a focus on traits or behaviours to a results-oriented approach has seen the emergence of objective-setting as a key issue.

However, rather than seeking to *set* objectives, managers would be better advised to attempt to *agree* objectives with their staff. Thus, during the course of the appraisal process the manager and employee should seek to agree objectives for the forthcoming period which comply with the mnemonic SMARTS.

S pecific

M easurable

A chievable

R ealistic

T imebound

S tretching

Which of the following two objectives is SMARTS?

1 To improve supervisory skills by taking responsibility for the training and development of a new trainee over the coming year.

2 To research, design, and implement a new sickness absence monitoring system that differentiates between certified and uncertified absences and that records frequency, duration, and reasons for absence. (This new system would be linked into a company-wide initiative to reduce costs by appropriate absence management techniques.) The budget for this exercise is x, the ongoing maintenance costs should be limited to two clerical labour hours a month, and the time-scale for implementation is y months.

The first example is not SMARTS because it is not specific and its outcomes would be difficult to measure. However, the second example provides a *specific* task with several *measurable* outcomes for the evaluation of success. The objective is presumably (barring disasters) *achievable* and *realistic* for the employee working with available resources, and is clearly *timebound*. It would also be *stretching* if it involved the employee in areas of work that he or she would not normally encounter in their day-to-day activities. Thus he or she would be able to build on new experiences and develop new skills. This individual objective is also clearly linked to an organisational goal: cutting costs.

Obviously, not all objectives can be defined in this way, because many lean more to qualitative rather than quantitative measurement, which is necessarily more subjective. Nevertheless, the mnemonic SMARTS provides an ideal to which you should aspire as far as possible.

We shall now return to considering performance appraisal in general terms by looking at the benefits of a well-designed and implemented scheme before we summarise best-practice issues.

Benefits of performance appraisal

Employees are often suspicious of new or revised appraisal schemes, particularly during times of rapid change or rationalisation. If you are faced with the task of introducing a new or updated scheme, you should pick your timing carefully, because many employees (sometimes rightly) view such innovations as a cynical way of selecting candidates for redundancy. As a consequence, many employers (particularly in the educational field) have sought to shift the emphasis from an appraisal approach (current performance) to a developmental approach (future needs).

In any event, if the design incorporates the list of key points provided in the section above on the components of performance appraisal schemes, the benefits for both the organisation and the individual should include the items listed in Table 8.

Table 8 Benefits of performance appraisal

For the organisation	For the individual
Improved communication of business goals	Increased understanding of strategic aims and own role in organisational success
Improvements in work performance and therefore overall business performance via, for example, increased productivity or customer service	Increased motivation

Increased job satisfaction |
| Identification of potential to aid succession planning | Development of potential

Better informed career-planning |
Training provision or development activities targeted at identified needs rather than provided on an *ad hoc* or 'first come first served' basis	Increased ability to meet own individual objectives as well as wider department or business objectives
Evaluation of effectiveness of selection criteria for new or newly promoted employees	Opportunity to publicise ambition
More objective distribution of rewards	Better understanding of the link between effort, performance, and reward
Improved retention of employees	Employability security

The above benefits demonstrate why organisations should seriously consider the value of introducing performance appraisal, but they should also bear in mind the many potential pitfalls. A half-hearted attempt to introduce formal performance appraisal may be more damaging in the long run than no attempt at all.

The training videos in this field usually present excellent 'good' and 'bad' practice scenarios for comparison (see the end of this chapter for recommended titles). The examples of bad practice may be considered extreme, used for their entertainment value only, but there are indeed many genuine horror stories to relate regarding employees' experiences of performance appraisal.

In order to help you to avoid the pitfalls suffered by some performance appraisal schemes, we have summarised a list of best-practice features.

Best practice in performance appraisal
Performance appraisal should incorporate the following:

- support from top management

- systems that are open and participative

- agreement at all levels about the purpose(s) of the scheme

- separation of reward reviews from the appraisal interviews

- clear, specific, and well-communicated (SMARTS) objectives which are jointly agreed

- line managers' recognition of their role in this process ie not seen as a personnel function

- clear link to the disciplinary procedure when handling poor performance so that the messages to the employee are the same

- training for appraisers *and* appraisees

- a 'maintenance' programme to ensure that follow-up action is taken eg training or development programmes are arranged as agreed

- a flexible culture to cater for individual and organisational needs

- simple administrative procedures

- consistency in managers' reporting standards

- formal regular appraisals and interim informal reviews between managers and their staff regarding performance and progress.

Throughout the discussion of performance appraisal above we have been touching on the related issue of reward and, more particularly, payment systems. We shall now examine this topic further.

PAYMENT SYSTEMS

UK organisations have in recent years tended to move away from the incremental salary systems established in the 1970s, and performance-related pay (PRP) is nowadays the dominant force. PRP is, however, another of those terms which mean different things to different people. The Institute of Personnel Management (now the IPD) provided a useful definition on this subject:

> Performance-related pay is the explicit link of financial reward to individual, group or company performance (or any combination of the three)... The principal types of performance-related pay are merit pay, individual

incentives, group/company performance bonuses and other variable payments which employees may earn which are related to team performance improvements.

(IPM 1990 : 1)

Thus, payment systems such as salaries, fixed hourly rates and, if we concentrate only on cash rewards, profit-related pay and profit-sharing are not included.

We stated earlier in this chapter that if a PMS is to be successful, then each and every aspect of it (or each 'intervention', to use Mike Walters' term) must be clearly linked and work towards the overall aim of continually improving business performance. This can be achieved only through your employees, who will expect to be rewarded for their loyalty, hard work, and contribution both *extrinsically* (factors generated by others) via promotions, salary, fringe benefits, bonuses, stock options etc and *intrinsically* (self-generated factors) via feelings of achievement, responsibility, personal growth, competence etc. The satisfactory integration of reward into the PMS is undoubtedly a difficult thing to achieve – not least because the factors that motivate employees vary from individual to individual. Further, for each individual, motivating factors fluctuate in their importance according to the changing circumstances of their lives. There is even disagreement about whether some extrinsic rewards have any motivational impact at all, but here we shall proceed on the assumption that they do have a short-term effect in increasing effort and, therefore, productivity.

In the context of performance management, we are concerned with the types of payment system available to organisations to encourage their employees to make worthwhile contributions towards the achievement of business goals. Armstrong and Murlis (1991: 282) state that for payment systems to act as real incentives to employees they must satisfy three basic requirements:

• that the reward should bear a direct relation to the effort

• that the payment should follow immediately or soon after the effort

• that the method of calculation should be simple and easily understood.

Thus payment systems such as salaries, fixed hourly rates and profit-sharing do not satisfy all of the above requirements. Many PRP schemes are however designed to succeed on all three counts. For instance, merit pay schemes may provide salary or wage increases in recognition of excellent job performances during the review period, and incentive or bonus schemes may provide payments in addition to base salary or wages related to the satisfactory completion of a project or the achievement of an individual or group target.

But PRP is not without its problems, mainly because of the difficulties encountered in trying to measure objectively individual or team performance and in establishing the most appropriate pay-out levels. For instance, working hard all year to be eligible for a maximum merit award of 4 per cent would probably be less motivating than seeking to achieve, say, three specific targets and a bonus payment of 10 to 20 per cent. Further, as stated in the IPM Factsheet (IPM 1990: 4):

Consideration needs to be given to the balance of variable and non-variable pay; rewards for individual, team and organisation contributions; discretionary rewards and rewards triggered automatically; cash rewards and non-cash rewards; and current and deferred pay.

The main lesson to be learnt here is that inclusion of a payment system such as PRP is not essential to the success of a PMS. However, where PRP is badly conceived or designed, it is unlikely to deliver the results expected and may threaten the whole standing of the PMS. With careful thought PRP can be introduced as an effective strategic tool linked to business needs, but it should not be relied upon as the sole motivator for employees: a PMS requires the right combination of financial and non-financial motivators.

Before progressing any further we must now pay careful attention to the legal considerations in this area.

LEGAL CONSIDERATIONS

It would appear at first sight that there is no specific legislation relating to performance appraisal issues. Yet Appendix 1 of the ACAS Advisory Handbook No 11, *Employee appraisal*, reproduced on page 120, leaves little room for doubt concerning the relevance of certain legal considerations.

Clearly the legislative background to performance appraisal is fairly complicated. Further, you should be aware that when dealing with poor performers there is an important link between the disciplinary procedure and the appraisal system. Large organisations may in fact have a separate capability procedure to cover this eventuality.

We have already said that managers are often loath to tackle poor performance as part of the appraisal process. There may be a temptation to duck the issue entirely and, for example, rate the employee concerned as 'satisfactory'. It is not difficult to imagine the reaction of all concerned when, shortly afterwards, formal action is taken to warn the employee of the consequences if a significant improvement in performance is not seen within the following three months.

This area is a complex one, but the ACAS Advisory Handbook *Discipline at work* provides excellent guidance on how to handle problems concerning poor performance; it is essential reading in this area.

We shall next consider the role of personnel practitioners in designing, administering, maintaining, and evaluating performance appraisal within their organisations.

THE ROLE OF PERSONNEL PRACTITIONERS

Personnel practitioners adopt a multifaceted role in the area of performance appraisal and within the wider remit of performance management within their organisations. Those of you in generalist roles are likely to get involved, with varying degrees of support from outside consultants, in a number of the following stages:

• identifying the need for a new or revised scheme

• designing the scheme

Appraisal – the legal considerations

Employers who recognise trade unions are required (if requested by the union) to disclose information[1] for the purposes of collective bargaining. In these circumstances, particularly where merit pay schemes are in operation, they may be requested to explain how appraisal systems operate and to describe the criteria against which employees are rated.

The Data Protection Act[2] gives individual employees a legal right to access to personal data (such as appraisal details) held about them on computers. 'Personal data' includes not just factual information but also opinions expressed about employees. Therefore employees could have access to opinions recorded about their performance or attitude at an appraisal. However, any indication of intentions, such as an intention to promote, is outside the scope of the Act. Manual personnel records are not covered by the legislation *(though this may change in the near future)*.

Under the Race Relations and Sex Discrimination Acts employees who feel that they have been refused promotion or access to training on grounds of their race or sex have the right to make a complaint to an industrial tribunal. In such cases appraisal forms and procedures may be used by employees to support their complaints. It is important therefore for employers to regularly monitor their appraisal systems and promotion policies to ensure that criteria used to assess performance are non-discriminatory in terms of both race and sex *(see Addendum below)*.

The Commission for Racial Equality (CRE) recommends[3] that staff responsible for performance appraisals should be told not to discriminate on racial grounds. The Equal Opportunities Commission (EOC) recommends[4] that appraisal systems should also assess actual performance in the job (which is not affected by the sex of the job holder). The EOC further advises employers to ensure that women are not rated lower than men who are performing at a comparable level.

---

(1) See ACAS Code of Practice No 2, *Disclosure of information to trade unions for collective bargaining purposes*

(2) See The Data Protection Act 1984 (Questions and Answers on the Act) – The Data Protection Registrar

(3) CRE *Race relations code of practice*

(4) EOC *Guidelines for equal opportunities for equal opportunities employers*

Addendum

In accordance with the Disability Discrimination Act 1995, employers should also ensure that they do not treat a disabled person less favourably than someone else because of their disability. This applies to all employment matters including recruitment, training, promotion and dismissal. Therefore, in the context of performance appraisal, employers must ensure that they regularly monitor their appraisal systems and access to training and promotion policies to ensure that criteria used to assess performance are non-discriminatory in terms of race, sex, and disability. In the case of disability, employers are further required to make reasonable changes to the workplace or the way the work is done to help the disabled person to do the job. Employers need to be very careful that their appraisal scheme does enable a fair judgement of the disabled person's abilities to be made. Many existing schemes are currently being revised to comply with this legislation.

- implementing and communicating the scheme

- designing and organising training for appraisers and appraisees

- administering the scheme

- monitoring the scheme

- maintaining the scheme (ie is it working efficiently?)

- evaluating the scheme (ie is it working effectively and does it meet its objectives?).

You will thus carry out all or some of the following roles (or possibly assist outside consultants in undertaking their roles).

A research role
This covers the various types of scheme in other organisations, their purposes, and link to the achievement of business objectives etc. (See the previous section on the components of performance appraisal schemes.)

A creative role
The aim here is to design a scheme which is tailored to your organisational circumstances and the needs of your employees.

An influencing role
The purpose of this role is to 'sell' the benefits of the scheme to senior managers, to the line managers who will be operating it, and to each and every employee who will be appraised.

A training role
This may cover the design, organisation, and delivery of training for both appraisers and appraisees regarding their familiarisation with the scheme and the skills of appraisal interviewing.

An administrative role
This involves implementing the scheme, communicating with all those affected at each stage, and ensuring that all the paperwork flows through the system according to the requisite time-scales, and that action points are followed up.

An advisory role
Advice has to be given to managers regarding, for example, developmental opportunities for their staff.

A monitoring role
You need to oversee consistency in applying standards, allocating rewards, and ensuring appeals are handled fairly and constructively.

Maintenance and evaluation roles
These ensure that the scheme continues to enjoy a high priority and that feedback on the success of the scheme (in reaching its objectives) is acted upon in amending, updating, and enhancing it.

An appraisal role
This is both as an *appraiser* for your own staff and as an *appraisee* in your own right. Further, if your organisation operates a 360-degree appraisal scheme, you may be involved as the neutral third party to provide feedback to a number of employees on the collated information provided by all the stakeholders involved in the process. (See Figure 8, page 113.)

INTERVIEWING SKILLS

Chapter 4 provides general guidance on interviewing techniques and skills. The majority of these are also applicable in an appraisal situation, although the purposes of appraisal interviews are of course different from selection interviews. Below we shall be concentrating on the skills necessary to be an effective appraiser.

We shall tackle appraiser skills by referring to the 'Dos and Don'ts' of appraisal interviewing: see Table 9.

SUMMARY

In this chapter we have sought to distinguish between the broad concept of performance management and the part played by performance appraisal within this framework. We have also explored the importance of the link between individual objectives and business goals, and have concluded that a lack of integration is the major stumbling-block towards a truly effective PMS for many organisations.

Performance appraisal has been examined in detail – its purposes, motivational effect, and history and trends. The differing components of performance appraisal schemes have been highlighted, including those involving the setting of objectives, and the major benefits and best-practice issues have been detailed.

Payment systems have been considered in general terms and, in the concluding sections, the legal considerations, the role of personnel practitioners, and the skills necessary to be an effective appraiser have been identified.

You will by now be familiar with the terms used and will be able to relate your learning to the scheme or schemes with which you are familiar. References, further readings, and recommended video titles are provided at the end of this chapter for your information, and the usual Activities section follows. You are encouraged to complete some, if not all, of these activities in order to reinforce and apply your learning.

ACTIVITIES

1 Find out as much as you can about the appraisal scheme(s) used by your organisation. Investigate the paperwork, talk to your manager and other line managers, talk to other employees, and use other learning sources to compare your practices with those of outside organisations. Then answer the eight questions set out under the 'Components of Performance Appraisal Schemes' section.

2 Following on from Activity 1, suggest some improvements that could be made to the scheme(s) operating in your workplace. Present them in the form of a written report to senior management, making sure that you justify your proposals.

3 Think about your own job role and what you would like to achieve over the next 12 months. Write down three to six key objectives for this period. Make sure that the majority of them tie in with business goals and that they all comply with the SMARTS guidelines.

Table 9 Appraisal interviewing – the appraiser

	Do	Don't
Before	• give the appraisee notice of the meeting and any preparation necessary • book a suitable venue • allow sufficient time • check on development opportunities • read the job description • review past appraisals and achievement of objectives • review performance over the whole period • collect facts and examples • consider future objectives • plan the agenda	• wait for the formal appraisal interview to tackle performance issues (good or bad) • be swayed by the 'halo or horns' effect ie when one feature exhibited by the appraisee governs your perception of their overall abilities. An example of the 'halo' effect would be a belief that because an employee has a business studies degree she is highly numerate. On the other hand, the 'horns' effect would apply when you assume that an employee who is persistently untidy lacks commitment and is unproductive. The beliefs may be correct but need to be verified by more objective methods • be overly influenced in your assessment by recent events
During	• state the purpose of the interview • invite the appraisee's views on his or her own performance • keep notes • praise strengths and discuss areas for improvement • listen • ask open and probing questions • jointly seek solutions • agree an action plan and future objectives • end on a positive note	• be afraid to tackle difficult issues • be bullied • concentrate on weaknesses at the expense of strengths • concentrate on personality issues at the expense of results • make assumptions eg about ambitions • argue • give vague responses to questions • make false promises • impose future objectives
Afterwards	• complete and return paperwork • ensure follow-up to action points • carry out regular reviews • hold frequent discussions *re* progress.	• file the papers and give the matter no more thought until the next review!

4   If you are inexperienced in appraisal interviewing – either as an appraiser or as an appraisee – set up a role-play situation with a like-minded individual so that you can both practise and receive feedback on your skills in appraisal interview situations. (See Table 9 and the video titles on page 124, which give guidance on appraiser and appraisee skills.)

REFERENCES AND FURTHER READING

The following are available from the Advisory, Conciliation and Arbitration Service (ACAS), ACAS Reader Ltd, P.O. Box 16, Earl Shilton, Leicester, LE9 8ZZ; tel. 01455 852 225:

Advisory booklet on appraisal-related pay. (Undated) Leicester, ACAS.

Advisory handbook on discipline at work. (Amended 1989) Leicester, ACAS.

Advisory booklet on employee appraisal. (Undated) Leicester, ACAS.

ARMSTRONG M. *and* MURLIS H. (1991) *Reward management: a handbook of remuneration strategy and practice.* 2nd ed. London, IPM and Kogan Page.

BEVAN S. *and* THOMPSON M. (1991) 'Performance management at the crossroads'. *Personnel Management.* November. pp36-9.

The following is available from Croner Publications Ltd, Croner House, London Road, Kingston-upon-Thames, Surrey, KT2 6SR; tel. 0181 547 3465:

Croner's personnel assistant's handbook. Kingston-upon-Thames, Croner Publications.

EGAN G. (1995) 'A clear path to peak performance'. *People Management.* 18 May. pp34–7.

GILLEN T. (1995) *The appraisal discussion.* London, Institute of Personnel and Development.

HALE R. *and* WHITLAM P. (1995) *Target setting and goal achievement.* London, Kogan Page.

INSTITUTE OF PERSONNEL MANAGEMENT. (1990) *IPM Factsheet No. 30: Performance-related pay.* London, Institute of Personnel Management.

INSTITUTE OF PERSONNEL MANAGEMENT. (1992) *Performance management in the UK: an analysis of the issues.* London, Institute of Personnel Management.

PETERS T. J. *and* WATERMAN R. H. (1982) *In search of excellence.* London, Harper and Row.

WALTERS M. (ed). (1995) *The performance management handbook.* London, Institute of Personnel and Development.

ACTS OF PARLIAMENT AND CODES OF PRACTICE

See page 120 for reference to relevant legislative acts and codes of practice.

VIDEOS

The dreaded appraisal. (1990) Video Arts (showing both sides of the appraisal interview).

The appraisal interview. (1994) Melrose Arts (showing both sides of the appraisal interview).

8 Personnel information systems

INTRODUCTION

In this chapter we shall look at the importance of records to the personnel function by examining the four main reasons for needing to keep them. Computers are playing an increasingly important role in personnel departments. We shall therefore consider the reasons for this and the benefits computers can offer to personnel practitioners. Remembering that personnel departments exist to serve the needs of the business, we shall consider how computers can assist in that objective. Then, to help with understanding the capability of computers, there is a section that lists the wide variety of purposes for which they can be used.

It is very likely that you will be called on to use a computer system, if not now, then in the foreseeable future. Indeed, you may be the main user of such a system. So you will want to have a say in choosing a new system or in the development of any existing system. To help you, we shall look at how a personnel practitioner might prepare to computerise an information system. This involves an appreciation of some of the technical aspects and of the implications of setting up the system. Lastly we shall look at the need to meet the requirements of the Data Protection Act 1984.

A glossary of terms is provided at the end of the chapter; you should refer to this for explanation of any terms with which you might be unfamiliar. In this chapter, computer terms that appear in the glossary are put in italics on the first occasion on which they are used.

THE IMPORTANCE OF PERSONNEL RECORDS

There are four main reasons why records are important: to satisfy legal requirements; to provide the organisation with information to make decisions; to record contractual arrangements and agreements; and to keep contact details of employees.

To satisfy legal requirements
Employment protection rights demand that we keep records to protect ourselves, as employers, from claims that we have discriminated against or unfairly dismissed employees. Health and safety legislation demands that records are kept of accidents, exposure to hazardous substances, training provided, and much more. Employers must be able to demonstrate responsible management of health and safety issues. Additionally, Government departments, including the Inland Revenue, can demand

information on how many people you employ, what they are paid and, indeed, what they have been paid over a number of years.

A glance at Chapter 3 will highlight the many legal requirements on organisations.

To provide the organisation with information to make decisions
Knowledge and information are the life-blood of good decision-making for organisations. For individuals, access to accurate, factual, and dependable information that can be used for arguments and influence is a vital factor in their ability to achieve. In the past, financial information has been highly regarded and available at considerable levels of sophistication. Personnel information has been harder to obtain but, because computers are moving into this arena, such information is becoming better and more readily available.

It is also significant that, in an era of high technology, products of all kinds are quickly and easily imitated. Consequently products are becoming increasingly similar and therefore business is beginning seriously to value service. It is now service that frequently differentiates one supplier from another. This leads to business decision-makers appreciating their employees' value more, because of this need for them to give good service to customers. In a healthy organisation 'good service' includes internal customers (ie fellow employees). In turn this places more emphasis on good personnel information.

To record contractual arrangements and agreements
Agreements that are recorded are clearer and also easier to insist upon. As well as it being a legal requirement to provide written particulars of employment, it is simply good practice to provide them. Employment problems are less likely to arise when all parties are clear about what has been agreed. Records are needed for reference purposes in the case of disputes and for defence if, for example, claims are made to an industrial tribunal.

To keep contact details of employees
The simplest and most obvious reason for this is so they can be paid. It is not difficult to see other reasons, such as the need to call someone in at short notice to provide relief cover.

Good organisation of records is the key to efficiency and effectiveness.

MANUAL AND COMPUTERISED RECORDS

You can see from the above that many records are kept and that many of these will be manual records ie written or printed on sheets of paper. It is unlikely, as a general rule, that application forms, copies of qualification certificates, and everyday correspondence received about an employee will be computerised. Such documents can be scanned into computers using special *scanners*, but they currently demand expensive equipment or expensive storage space on computer *hard disks*. The advantage of having scanned documents on computer is that they can then be accessed by means of a computer screen rather than by going to a filing cabinet. However, unlike other *data*, their contents cannot be easily *processed* or indexed without further work. Consequently the advantage of computerising such documents is limited.

Nonetheless, much personnel information does lend itself to computerisation, and increasingly so. To understand why, envisage this experiment: look up your own telephone number in the directory. So long as you have an entry, you will find that quite easy. Now change one digit at the end of the number. Can you find whose number that is? Theoretically it is possible, but it would be an inordinately difficult task, and the number may not even exist. By comparison, if the directory was on computer disk, the task could take seconds or even less. That is because a computer *database* can *search* on a whole variety of different indexed *fields*. Once a database has been set up for employees, you may be able to find who is due for a long-service award, who will retire next year, whose probationary period ends next week, whose salary exceeds £30,000 – just by searching the appropriate field.

This is only one example of the power of the computer. So what other benefits are there?

BENEFITS TO PERSONNEL OF COMPUTERS

Computers make the management, and in particular the analysis, of information much more efficient. In doing so they offer new opportunities that (as we have just seen) would not be practical with manual systems. To be valuable, information should be meaningful and should assist the making of decisions. For example, an employee's attendance *record* might provide information that makes a disciplinary warning appropriate. Providing valuable information in a timely fashion is very important for the credibility of the personnel function.

Computers enable administrative tasks to be monitored and completed more effectively. A good recruitment system, for example, will acknowledge applications, prompt timely action, keep track of the progress of individual applications, facilitate letters of invitation to interview, and prepare the letters of rejection. Finally it can transfer details of successful candidates to the main record system. Word processing of standard letters, or standard paragraphs, and the *mail-merging* of addresses make essential communications easier, and it becomes practical to personalise far more correspondence.

The use of processing facilities in databases and spreadsheets enables what would be laborious calculations to be completed in a timely fashion. This can assist in wages and salary negotiation, the calculation of increased salaries, redundancy pay calculations, and many others. In wages bargaining, for example, *what-if models* can quickly calculate the cost to the organisation of an extra penny on shift allowance or an extra 1 per cent on the basic salary rate.

Computers have come to personnel rather later than to accounts or payroll, which is largely owing to the complexity of the personnel function. There is also a wide variation in the information needs of different organisations. Personnel *applications* also tend to need significant amounts of text compared with accounts or payroll, therefore demanding more hard-disk space. Today, the lower costs of high-capacity computers, the availability of inexpensive and fast letter-quality printers, and the increasing amount of sophisticated *software* specifically geared to the personnel function has brought, and will continue to bring, about great change.

Before looking at the many applications of computers in the personnel function it is worth considering the benefits. If your organisation does not have a personnel computer system, you will probably want to make a case for one. On the other hand, if you already have a system, it is likely you will want to continue to build on it. Don't lose sight of the reasons for your wants! Computers in the personnel function are not an end in themselves but a means to better business performance. Try to distinguish between what you need (the software to produce organisation charts, perhaps) and an item which you would like (a notebook with a colour screen, maybe) but which will not enhance business performance.

BENEFITS TO THE BUSINESS OF COMPUTERS IN PERSONNEL

Timeliness

As the pace of change in organisations continues to increase, decision-makers are demanding more information more quickly than in the past. By way of illustration, think about negotiators in the annual pay round. If the cost of a particular settlement option can be assessed quickly, then time spent in negotiation will be reduced. If supervisors are to be effective in tackling poor attendance, it has to be identified and acted on quickly. Computers make it possible to have 'trigger levels'. Trigger levels mean that as soon as a particular employee's 'number of days absent' exceeds a set level the matter is flagged up and a supervisor can be prompted to assess the situation.

Always remember, of course, that for the computer to produce timely information (flagging up the poor attender in our example) it has to have the 'raw data' in the first place. Thus staff (data input clerks, perhaps) will be needed for the attendance records to be *input* to the computer first. If the input is not timely the computer will be of no help. Ideally the data could come from another computer source; in our example that might be the payroll. Putting any data onto a computer system once only is an ideal to strive for. Unfortunately, computer links between payroll and personnel systems are often difficult to make.

Accuracy

Once a correct piece of data is put onto a computer system then, unless changed by a deliberate (or accidental) process, it stays correct. It can be used for calculations or transferred to other applications without change. Dates of birth are just one example. In the personnel department they can be used to calculate age (updating it every time it is looked at) or transferred to another application, such as pensions administration. Similarly, once a calculation has been set up using the correct logic, it can be performed easily and accurately every time. For example, redundancy calculations usually require a date of birth, the date on which service commenced, and current earnings (the raw data). The calculations are often complex. Nonetheless, once set up on a computer, accurate data can be accessed and consistent redundancy calculations completed with confidence and timeliness. Don't forget the importance of the original data being accurate! Equally, the logic of any processes performed on the data has to be correct.

Again, accuracy depends on the operator and (for the calculations) the programmer. However, the computer can assist by rejecting, or asking for confirmation of, what might be errors. As an example, it could reject (by means of messages on the input screen) a date of birth that suggests an employee is too young or ask for confirmation if the employee is over retirement age.

Presentation

We all tend to believe the printed word in preference to hand-written notes. Indeed, in formal business correspondence presentation generates credibility. Just reflect on how much paper flows onto your desk with the morning mail. How do you decide what to read? Leaving aside essential communications, visual impression is a major factor. You are more likely to read a document that is visually interesting. Often it is only parts of a document that may be relevant to you, so you will want to be able to identify what is important to read. You will probably distrust the authority of material that is riddled with spelling mistakes or grammatical errors. Are you impressed with material that uses old-fashioned or inappropriate type styles? What impression is given of the writer by lack of attention to detail or to style?

We hope you will agree that, in seeking to influence others, presentation is a major factor. Crucially, personnel practitioners have many people to influence. Think about the senior manager who has requested information, the promising candidate assessing whether she wants to work for you, the neighbour who has written to complain about noise from your factory. Modern printers produce letter quality that rivals commercial typesetting and can provide colour print and diagrams. Most word processors have scaleable *fonts* and can incorporate photographs and other attractive features. Desktop publishers have so many features that they can be used for brochures, newsletters, and sophisticated overhead projector slides.

To use these facilities demands an investment in learning, and the result still depends on the skill of the operator. In general, the more sophisticated the presentation, the more investment is needed in learning and the more time is required to produce the final document. Remember, therefore, to keep the standard of presentation in line with your purpose. As course tutors, we see too many written assignments with distinction-level presentation but barely passable content. You cannot influence by presentation alone!

Flexibility

Sophisticated systems allow a great deal of flexibility in how information is analysed and presented. Often they make it practical to carry tasks and information that would be too laborious to collate, analyse, and present by using manual systems. For instance, it is now practical to calculate the actual cost of a particular salary review settlement on a what-if basis (see glossary).

The main source of inflexibility in computer systems is the difficulty of incorporating variations. Computers lend themselves rather better to inflexible, standard processes than to flexible, *ad hoc* responses. As an example, you might reflect on letters of 'rejection' where applicants and candidates are turned down. Standardisation in such a letter will often be obvious to the candidate, and yet standardisation (where the same activity is repeated again and again) is an area in which computers are highly valuable. You will have to learn to strike a balance between efficiency and impression.

Administrative efficiency

Fortunately, much administration is repetition of an activity again and again. As an example, consider the recruitment and selection process. From the point an application form is sent out, the applicant's address will be used several times: to send out the form, to acknowledge the application if it is returned, subsequently to decline the application or to invite for interview, then to decline or offer an appointment, and perhaps finally to go on the employee's records file. Many of the communications will need to be standardised, especially in a major recruitment exercise, and you will also need to keep track of how each applicant progresses. Nonetheless, one recruitment exercise is, in administrative terms, fundamentally the same as another. Not surprisingly this is an area in which computerisation can save considerable time. The value to the organisation is reduced time for filling the vacancy and lower administration costs.

Remember that time is needed to learn the system and, as already highlighted, overstandardisation is not ideal in the sensitive area of recruitment.

Accessibility of personnel information

Computers make information accessible. It is now possible to have every piece of frequently used information stored on a single personal computer (PC), or central *server*, with a keyboard and screen on your desk. It makes it easier and faster to respond to *ad hoc* enquiries. Salary enquiries are one example. Typically, in manual systems, a salary card with salary history is held for every employee in an individual wallet and stored in a filing cabinet. Obtaining one salary is a minor inconvenience. Thirty salaries would be a major interruption. On a computer screen neither would be a serious problem and sophisticated systems make it easy to print out 'hard copy' ie print the salaries onto a sheet of paper. This is less prone to error than copying figures from salary cards.

Of course, salaries are typical of information that we need to keep confidential. Indeed, the Data Protection Act 1984 specifically binds us to avoid unregistered disclosure of information. Passwords, careful placing of computer display screens (so visitors cannot pry), and simply locking the computer, and office, at night are appropriate precautions. Many personnel practitioners resist *networked* computers with unrestricted access, where security becomes dependent solely on passwords. Unfortunately, the value of interchanging data, with accounts systems for example, is a counter-force. It creates pressure to share company-wide networked systems.

Multiple access

There are advantages indeed in less restricted access. For example, where line managers can access information about their subordinates without directly involving personnel staff they are more likely to do so. Better management decisions are likely to result. Interruptions in a personnel office are a major source of inefficiency. Therefore a networked system that allows enquirers to answer their own queries will help personnel practitioners to make greater contributions in other areas of expertise.

In terms of the politics in an organisation, knowledge and information are power. Not all personnel practitioners are comfortable with making this more easily accessible. It may reduce their own ability to influence others because it reduces the opportunity to divulge information selectively!

Staff performance

Reference information on matters such as employment legislation and training material on almost any business subject are becoming readily available through computer facilities. This means better-informed personnel staff. When used for training such material creates the potential for greater performance from all employees in their job areas. Wider availability means that decisions and plans for the future can make much greater use of factual information.

LOOKING AT THE NEED FOR A COMPUTER SYSTEM

One of the practical difficulties in understanding how best to use computers is that we need to use one first to understand what it will do. Although we can envisage all kinds of need in our personnel department, some understanding of computers is essential if we are to know whether a computer solution would be viable. Once we own a computer system we might then realise that it is not a practical solution for our particular needs. Yet, at the same time, we might discover a host of other needs that the system could satisfy.

As an example, consider the purposes for which Sellotape is used. Those needs existed before it was invented. Once it had been invented, it was possible to establish whether Sellotape would meet those needs. If you have a roll of Sellotape in your house or office, you may find 'new' needs for it every day. For example, you may discover, perhaps by chance, its value in removing dog hairs from clothing!

Computers are of course a rather more significant investment. The costs of *hardware* and software are likely to require authorisation from senior levels in your organisation. The hidden cost of learning new systems, getting data onto the system, and modifying systems to your requirements may be even greater. So it makes sense to try to identify needs in advance rather than buying first and relying on a trial-and-error approach.

What might your organisation need?

The starting-point should be the end purposes that are to be satisfied. Here are some examples:

- Managers in organisations seek personnel information to make decisions – eg decisions about how to structure the organisation.

- Personnel information is also used for control – eg keeping salaries in line with labour market trends.

- Much of what the personnel function does is administrative – eg finding employees, and ensuring they are paid correctly and on time.

To achieve these objectives we need raw data ie records. Dates of birth, salaries, and attendances would all be examples of raw data. For this to become useful information it has to be processed (hence the term data-processing) so that it is meaningful. Age profiles, salary comparisons, and average attendance levels are examples of this raw data processed so as to be more meaningful.

If you have not done so already, you will soon have to familiarise yourself with computers to ascertain whether they might satisfy business needs. Computer and systems salesmen are inclined to suggest computers will satisfy any administrative or data-processing need, which is broadly true. However, what is crucially important is how economically and practically viable it might be to use a computer to satisfy a particular requirement. Always remember, too, that the raw data has to be available in a timely and reliable form and has to be input to the system before it can be processed.

Another approach to identifying the needs that computers may satisfy is to look at the specific things that computers can do. Returning to our Sellotape example, this is equivalent to researching the purposes for which others use Sellotape to identify tasks that it might do for us.

APPLICATIONS FOR COMPUTERS

You will have noticed that we have referred to the use to which a computer is put as an 'application'. Thus, drawing an organisation chart may be considered an application, and there is a variety of proprietary software available to meet this purpose. For clarity, this software is usually referred to as 'applications software'. Matching organisation needs to applications software demands a knowledge of both the needs and the software. So let's have a look and see what applications software is available to meet potential business needs. In doing so we may discover others that we would like to satisfy. Some priority-setting is likely to be necessary.

Word processing
This is probably the first computer application for many personnel departments. As well as being more productive than typing, it lends itself well to the standard correspondence typical of the personnel function. By use of facilities such as mail-merge and standard letters or paragraphs considerable efficiencies can be achieved. The various facilities for improving presentation that word processing provides may also be important to the department's credibility.

Primary employee records
This is another popular first application and is often a necessary first step. The data here would typically be personal details such as name, address, date commenced work, date of birth, National Insurance number, payroll number, and salary. It could be used in its raw, unprocessed form to send out a letter, for example. In addition it could be processed to identify who is due to retire or to calculate salary costs for a department. Aggregating data for reports to managers is a valuable computer task. Databases are frequently used for this purpose. Separate databases for past and present employees are common. Usually a computer *routine* transfers details from one database to the other.

Absence recording and analysis
This is another popular early application. Because tangible financial savings can be identified from reductions in absence level, it is easier to make a cost case for this application. Only actions taken by managers and supervisors can bring the absence level down, but good records can help them to do that job. The personnel department can also monitor the situation to see that the job is being done.

Administration
Much of the literature concentrates on computerised personnel information systems whereas, in fact, personnel departments are equally interested in reducing administrative burdens. Computers can help with many aspects of administration, of which recruitment administration is a particularly good example.

Spreadsheets
These are a handy application and are often included within the *bundle* when hardware is sold. They can be used to check pension calculations, prepare redundancy calculations, and for what-ifs in negotiations. They are most useful when rows and columns of figures need to be used for a series of repetitive calculations. However, for many personnel requirements, such calculations can be done within processes in other applications. A database may display a person's age on the computer screen, for example, by running a process that calculates age. Processes within applications tend to supersede spreadsheets.

Diaries
These can bring to your attention all the tasks to be done each day. They can identify which probationary periods need chasing, what long-service awards are due, when retirements are pending, which salary reviews are due – indeed anything that they are set up to identify.

A slightly different diary facility can bring together the diaries of different managers, making it much easier to identify dates and venues. This can be invaluable for discovering when, for example, all members of a recruitment panel might be available.

Payroll
Some people see this as the first personnel-related computer application. It contains much of the information held in primary records and for this reason there is a great temptation to amalgamate the two. Unfortunately, payrolls are designed for weekly (or monthly) calculations and for 'pay history' purposes. They do not usually lend themselves well to the task of providing or analysing other personnel information. It is possible to 'link' payroll and personnel systems, but because systems houses tend to specialise in one application or the other good 'links' are not easy to make.

Time and attendance
Systems such as these help manage flexi-time and, when linked to payroll, pay. Clocking systems are linked to a central computer and can make considerable administrative savings. Care is needed over who controls the system to ensure there is no abuse.

Organisation charts
Drawing organisation charts by hand is a long and tedious task and one that soon needs repeating if they are to be kept up to date. People outside the personnel function often ask why personnel practitioners never seem to be able to cope with what they see as an easy task. Fortunately, a variety of software now exists to make the task more manageable.

Candidate selection systems
These are a very different form of application, but there is a wide variety available. A number of purveyors of psychometric testing provide their

own software; others sell selection systems to help identify suitable candidates from your own employees. These are, obviously, more relevant to larger organisations.

Processing applications

Placing primary employee records onto a computer database provides in itself no more than a computerised reference system, valuable though that might be. Adding processing applications offers benefits by facilitating routine calculations. Complex calculations such as those for redundancy pay, pensions, labour turnover, salary trends, and time to fill vacancies can be set up and easily and routinely calculated. Furthermore, what-if calculations can be invaluable in assisting decision-making.

Training records

The key to effective training records is to identify what information is likely to be required and to code it effectively. Long descriptions of course titles are not helpful, and qualifications are very diverse and consequently difficult to code. Coding is important because merely searching to see who has been on a personnel course would not identify a course entitled 'Recruitment and Selection' or, even, 'Human Resource Management'. Nonetheless, there are some important benefits to be had from computerised records if they are coded effectively. At one extreme, it makes it possible to find who might entertain an important French-speaking visitor and at the other it facilitates the planning of an organisation's training strategy.

Other record systems

There are many other records that lend themselves to computerisation. Company vehicle records, Control of Substances Hazardous to Health records, and equal opportunities monitoring are just a few such. With interrelational databases they can usually be cross-referenced to the primary employee records and to each other.

Communication facilities

Computers offer the opportunity for much greater availability of information through *e-mail*, the *Internet* and *web pages*, *bulletin boards*, and computerised fax. These enable communication with many (or selected) employees by means of single actions. Bulletin boards make it easy to refer to reference material such as the disciplinary procedure. With e-mail you can trace whether your communication has been read and, with all these facilities, manage your communications. It makes it possible to refer back easily to what was said, to whom, and when, and, in some cases, to discover whether they did anything about it!

Reference systems

These make pertinent information available from huge quantities of data. Reference books such as some of those published by Croner are now available on disk, making it easy to search for any subject by using a key word. The IPD is investing in technology to provide access to information through the Internet; their address is http://www.ipd.co.uk. If you have a *CD-ROM* facility on a home computer you will probably already have come across ENCARTA™. This is an encyclopaedia available on a CD disk and may be read through your *CD-ROM drive*. Although expensive, many business and professional reference works are becoming available on CD-ROM. The cost of reference material on CD-ROM is certain to fall as the market expands.

Expert systems
As specialised versions of reference information, expert systems can guide inexperienced individuals (by means of question-and-answer sessions) through otherwise complex decisions. In personnel, such systems can be used to guide managers through disciplinary action and legal requirements.

Interactive learning
Similar in principle to expert systems, these often use CD-ROM and Laser disks to enable learning. Typically, users choose answers to questions posed and the system takes the user through learning points appropriate to the answers they give. Computer-based systems usually use text (or mainly text), CD-ROM includes a variety of illustrations, and Laser disks incorporate substantial amounts of video illustration.

PREPARING TO COMPUTERISE

It is likely that your organisation already has a personnel computer system. If so, then we suggest you study it carefully. Find out how it measures up both to the advantages and disadvantages described above. How many of the applications are available? Would you like to see any of the above applications introduced? Does your computer have other applications that are not described above?

If your organisation does not have a personnel computer system then perhaps it is an area of development that you can encourage.

Where to start
If you are contributing to the choice of a computer system or reviewing the effectiveness of the current one, start with your ability to meet your organisation's needs. For what information are you continually asked? To what discussions and decisions does your department regularly contribute? What would you like to influence? Personal networking would be a valuable step in answering this and for looking at options. Talk to others in your personal network group and find out what they do. Perhaps they will let you visit them, talk you through the system they have, and explain how it meets their needs.

People Management and other personnel publications generally have many advertisements for personnel systems. Bear in mind that some specialise in very large systems and others in smaller applications. Cautious contacts with these organisations will help you begin to appreciate what is available. If asked, most suppliers will visit you and give an on-site demonstration. However, if they do this without much commitment on your part, then they may be operating on quite high margins – ie the system could be expensive. Looking at literature or visiting exhibitions could be a better first step.

Observing demonstrations
Whether at an exhibition or on your premises, you should know what to look for in any demonstration. You would be wise to be cautious. The following list is not exhaustive, but it contains some key points you may wish to bear in mind:

- Ease of use is an important area in looking at a system.

- Make sure you understand what is happening at the demonstration.

- Check how many records the demonstration is using – is it comparable to the number of records you will need?

- Ask how to do some simple tasks that you might want to do yourself (eg a list of salaries in the accounts department).

- Ask how easy it is to tailor selections, reports, and routine activities to your own needs. (For example, how would it be if you wished to exclude the finance director's salary from the above list?)

- Is the software based on an *operating system* with which you are familiar. For example, is it based on Windows?

- Ask how the application might link up with existing software such as word processing or that in the accounts department or in payroll.

- Make sure you know on what hardware the demonstration is running. Run on different equipment it may well be slower.

Home-grown systems

If you are quite computer-literate you may be able to develop your own systems. With some of the *menu-driven* packages that help you write database applications, this is not unduly difficult, but it will be time-consuming. As a start it will give you much understanding of how these systems work and be invaluable in evaluating longer-term options.

In giving you an opportunity to demonstrate what can be done, it may help you to make the case for a proprietary system. However, unless you want to specialise in this area, home-grown systems are not a long-term solution because of the substantial time that they require. You will be also duplicating work that has been done, usually very effectively, by commercial software developers.

The next steps

Once you have some feel for systems, it would be wise to give careful thought as to what you would want a system to *do* for your department or organisation. Have a look back through the benefits and applications above and relate them directly to the needs you identified earlier. Choose that application or those applications that are likely to realise most benefits. Read through suitable literature on computer systems, especially computerised personnel systems. A single chapter in a book, such as this one, can only give you 'pointers'. Think through how a computer system might come about in your organisation. Do you have an information technology (IT) department? Who will be able to make the decision? Who will need to be convinced?

Now you know something about the subject you will want to talk to appropriate people in your organisation. We assume you will have influence in any decision but that the responsibility to purchase will be taken by a more senior person. Your influence will be greatest if you are quite clear about the benefits, the costs, and the type of system needed. Do recognise the importance of ease of use, especially if you are the person who will be using it!

TECHNICAL ASPECTS

The sort of equipment that applications will need – the hardware – will depend on the size of your organisation and the requirements of the applications. A good supplier will recommend the appropriate hardware but will expect you to have thought a little about your requirements.

Integration

Will your computer system need to integrate with other systems such as accounts, the payroll, or a mainframe? It could be that, given substantial computer capacity in the organisation, a stand-alone system is not appropriate.

Security

This covers not just password protection and the other issues we looked at under accessibility, but also long-term protection of data. The major threats are computer failure, viruses, fire, and even sabotage. The main protection against all these is a regular programme of *backups*. If this is to be done, then the backup system must be easy to operate. Make sure your supplier addresses this issue with an approach that is not unduly time-consuming. Keep the following in mind:

- Backups must be capable of being restored to a different machine to cover machine failures.

- Viruses usually come from software that originates from an uncertain source, such as pirated software; they might now also come through the Internet.

- Discipline in using only proprietary software helps, but anti-virus software is widely available and should be used.

- Backups are important in virus protection because if a virus does get through it may corrupt your data. In that case your only hope could be your last uncorrupted backup.

- Fire and sabotage can be covered by using a fireproof safe for backups or by an off-site backup (password-protected) at another location. If you are a 'belt and braces' person you will do both!

Networking

In a typical department more than one person will need access to the computer system at any given time. This can be achieved by a network of computers linked together using sophisticated software. You will have to decide if you require this and, if so, how many stations are needed. A further step would be for line managers in your organisation to be able to access data through an organisation-wide network. This is a major decision for the organisation to take.

Printers, ROM drives and other *peripherals*

What is needed will depend on your organisation size, department size, and the applications you are using. It is important to give some thought to these, guided, perhaps, by your supplier or by an information technology department.

SETTING UP A SYSTEM

This is a huge task, and one that can very easily be underestimated.

Because you cannot get information from the system until the data has been entered you need to do this first. There will be decisions to make about organising the data. For example, you will have to decide how to identify individuals; this could be by surname, clock number, National Insurance number, a special computer-generated number, or even all of these. The department and cost code structure of your organisation will be needed to segregate employees. This structure may be already well organised – or not organised at all!

In addition to details of existing employees, data on past employees could be relevant too. Often these will not be put on at the outset. Past employees' details are more easily generated when an employee leaves. Records for those who have already left at the time the system is introduced are usually kept as manual records.

The question as to who puts the data onto the computer can be a vexing one. To combine the task with everyday duties in a busy personnel department is not very practical. And yet there are confidentiality issues and current knowledge matters that surround the use of outside help. Some prefer the use of non-office hours (ie evenings and weekends) for a limited time, as the solution. The practicalities will need to be thought out carefully in each case.

DATA PROTECTION ACT 1984

If your organisation controls the use of personal data on a computer, it becomes a data-user; this applies the moment you hold such data on a computer. The Data Protection Act 1984 requires an organisation to register the fact that it is using data. It does not matter whether this data is 'sensitive' or not; a name and address would constitute personal data. Each purpose has to be registered; and if 'Personnel/employee administration' is a new purpose, it will need to be registered.

Registering
Registration is done by completing a form and requesting an entry on the data protection register. The entry is prepared from this form and remains in the public domain. It will give broad descriptions of:

- the data which you hold

- the purposes for which you hold it

- the sources from which you intend to obtain the information

- the people to whom you may wish to disclose the information

- overseas countries to which you may wish to transfer the data.

Data protection principles
As a data-user you have to comply with a set of principles that are designed to protect individuals from the misuse of data. These are summarised in Table 10 and are described in detail in a student pack that is available from the registrar; see the References and Further Reading section at the end of this chapter.

Table 10 The data protection principles

The first principle
'The information to be contained in personal data shall be obtained, and personal data shall be processed, fairly and lawfully.'

The second principle
'Personal data shall be held only for one or more specified and lawful purposes.'

The third principle
'Personal data held for any purpose or purposes shall not be used or disclosed in any manner incompatible with that purpose or those purposes.'

The fourth principle
'Personal data held for any purpose or purposes shall be adequate, relevant and not excessive in relation to that purpose or those purposes.'

The fifth principle
'Personal data shall be accurate and, where necessary, kept up to date.'

The sixth principle
'Personal data held for any purpose or purposes shall not be kept for longer than is necessary for that purpose or those purposes.'

The seventh principle
'An individual shall be entitled –
(a) at reasonable intervals and without undue delay or expense –
    (i) to be informed by any data user whether he holds personal data of which that individual is the subject; and
    (ii) to access to any such data held by a data user; and
(b) where appropriate to have such data corrected or erased.'

The eighth principle
'Appropriate security measures shall be taken against unauthorised access to, or alteration, disclosure or destruction of, personal data and against accidental loss or destruction of personal data.'

One particularly relevant provision is that appropriate security measures must be taken against unauthorised access to, or disclosure, alteration, or destruction of data. Personnel departments need to be particularly careful about disclosure, whether data is held on computer or not. Personnel computer screens should not be visible to visitors to the department. Keep in mind that telephone calls from people purporting to be building societies, future employers, or other plausible bodies may, in fact, be from private investigators.

Of course you will want to respond to genuine written enquiries. Therefore the intention to make such disclosures should be recorded in your data protection entry. It is also important to remember that having an entry does not oblige you to make a disclosure.

What are the legal implications?
It is a criminal offence to hold personal data without registering it, and your employer could be prosecuted. The same applies if the data is used outside the terms of its registration; in this case you as an employee could be prosecuted. However, this applies only if you have done this 'knowingly and recklessly' – but be careful!

Individuals have rights under the Act. They include the right to have access ('subject access') to the information you hold on them (although not to any intentions, such as promotion, that you may have). Failure to comply means that the individual can complain to the registrar, who has a range of powers. Individuals can also request information to be corrected or deleted, and they can also sue for damages if they suffer financial loss (or physical injury) as the result of incorrect data.

Another potential danger for the personnel department is being faced with a mass request for 'subject access'. To reduce this risk, and the risk of inaccuracy, some employers provide employees with a periodic printout of data held on them.

THE ROLE OF PERSONNEL PRACTITIONERS

Personnel information systems are tools which you use to support line managers and to assist with your other personnel roles and activities. We can look at your role in three categories.

An administrative role
This involves keeping well-organised records and providing information. It is seen by some as the dull area of personnel activities. However, the flow of information around an organisation is vital to effective decision-making. Providing the management of the organisation with quality personnel information (ie pertinent, clear, timely, and accurate) represents a major contribution to the business. At the same time, it is a substantial job for personnel practitioners, and one that can be underestimated far too easily.

An influencing role
In this role you are meeting the challenge of providing quality information that enhances the credibility of the personnel function in your organisation. Credibility leads to greater access to decision-makers. That makes your job more rewarding and may provide the opportunity to extend your role and influence into other interesting areas.

A user role
This concerns the user of computerised systems. Here you may become the customer of an IT department or of an external supplier. You will have a part to play in ensuring that the systems meet your needs for providing your 'customers' with the information they in turn need. Making sure that computers assist, rather than hinder, this objective is a substantial task in itself.

SUMMARY

We have looked at the need to keep records and at the benefits of computer systems both to the personnel function and the organisation. You should now have a broad idea of the range of applications to which a computer can be put and of what is involved in choosing and implementing a computer system. We have also considered the requirement to register with the Data Protection Registrar.

Computers are here to stay. The price of data storage space continues to fall, and computer capabilities to increase. In addition, the speed with which information can be communicated (eg via modems) is also increasing and its cost falling. Personnel practitioners need familiarity with computers, and the communication of information, to assess how these facilities can help them in their personnel responsibilities.

If you already have a system, still take time to keep up with the trends in improved software, new applications and communications.

ACTIVITIES

1 If you are not computer-literate then you should become so. The best way is to get your hands on a computer application at your workplace or a widely available computer application such as word processing or a spreadsheet. Find someone to guide you. Some members of courses we have run have been very expertly tutored by their children!

2 Access to information on computers and, particularly, the input of information to computers is done mainly through a keyboard. Irrespective of level in the organisation, you should be able to use a keyboard. So if you still type with two fingers, buy a suitable text or enrol on a short course and improve your skills.

3 Review how you currently manage information:

- Have a close look at the records in your department. Identify what is recorded, what duplications occur, what information is routinely sought, what information is aggregated. Is there data recorded that is never used? How much time does it take to record the data? How easy is it to obtain information when it is needed?

- What routines exist to ensure data is kept up to date? Do they work? How do systems cope with current information required before current data has been recorded?

- What would happen if there was a fire? Are critical pieces of data protected? If nothing is protected, what should be? Would you be able to get at key information (such as contact details) if access to the site was denied?

4 If you have a computer system, go through the questions on page 135 in the first paragraph of the Preparing to Computerise section.

5 Visit an exhibition and persuade exhibitors to show you their systems in a free demonstration.

6 The Data Protection Registrar provides a series of guidelines and a student pack. You might find it useful to obtain these and use them to check how your organisation is complying with the Act. You should be able to obtain a copy of your registration from within your organisation. If necessary, you can gently remind the person responsible that the registration entry is in the public domain.

GLOSSARY

The letters (q.v.) in brackets after a word mean that you can look up that word elsewhere in the glossary.

application   the use of a computer to carry out a specific, useful task. The term is sometimes used loosely to refer to the software (q.v.) involved in a computer application.

back-up   a copy of a file, or a complete hard disk (q.v.), held in case the original file or disk is corrupted or lost.

bulletin board   a store of information on a server (q.v.) that is available to a wide number of computer users (in which respect it is similar to a conventional notice board). Bulletin boards usually have available a number of facilities, for example the ability to supply software (q.v.) to other computers via a network (q.v.) or a modem (q.v.).

bundle   a computer purchase within which various items such as software (q.v.) and small peripherals (q.v.) may be included in one price.

CD-ROM   an optical storage disk for data; it looks like a domestic audio disc.

CD-ROM drive   a device for reading information on CD-ROM (q.v.) and transferring it to a computer.

data   unanalysed information coded and structured for subsequent processing (q.v.).

database   a collection of data which is organised in such a way that it may be accessed easily by a wide variety of applications (q.v.) programs. In one sense a telephone directory is a database – although not a very flexible one.

e-mail   an electronic system for transferring messages; it is usual for messages to be held in a central store for retrieval at the receiver's convenience.

field   a predetermined section of a record (q.v.) allocated to the storage of a particular data (q.v.) item eg date of birth.

font   a set of characters of a particular typeface, style, and size. Scaleable fonts can be varied in size by specifying that size in 'points' (a point is about 1/72nd of an inch).

hard disk   a rigid magnetic disk located with a machine that stores data (q.v.).

hardware   the physical components of a computer system, including peripherals (q.v.). It is usually supplied in metal cases, hence 'hard'.

Internet   a complex communication channel between computers all over the world.

input   presenting data (q.v.) to a computer so that it is converted into electrical impulses for storage or processing (q.v.); usually done with a keyboard.

mail-merge   adding stored addresses etc to standard-format word-processed documents so as to personalise them.

menu   a list of optional procedures displayed on a computer screen from which the user can select an appropriate item.

menu-driven a software (q.v.) program written, or operated, by selecting options from a menu (q.v.).

modem a device that converts audio tones (eg telephone transmission) into digital (computer) form and vice versa for transmission over telephone-type circuits.

network a linked set of computers or systems capable of sharing computer power or storage facilities. Don't confuse this with your own personal network of contacts – the term is used in both senses within the chapter.

operating system a set of programs that controls the operation of the computer. DOS and Windows are common examples of operating systems; there are a number of others.

output information coming out of a computer after processing (q.v.).

peripheral an input (q.v.) (eg a keyboard), output (q.v.) (eg a printer), or storage device (eg a CD-ROM driver (q.v.)).

processing in the context of this chapter this is the term used to describe an operation in which a computer performs a series of calculations or a series of logical deductions, for example calculating someone's age or deciding who is due for a long-service award.

record a collection of related items of data (q.v.), treated as a unit for processing (q.v.). Typically you would hold one record for every employee.

routine a set of program instructions performing a particular task, but not a complete program.

scanner a device used to input data (q.v.) into a computer. In the context of this chapter it means a device that is passed over a paper image to create a computerised graphic version of the document. (Fax machines incorporate scanners, except that the paper is passed through and the scanner is static.)

searching attempting to find particular data (q.v.) within a file or database (q.v.) eg telephone sales units often search for enquirers' addresses by postcode.

server a hard disk (q.v.) used to serve (ie provide) more than one computer with stored data (q.v.).

software programs, routines (q.v.), and procedures that can be implemented on a computer system; originally provided on paper tape or floppy disks, hence 'soft'.

spreadsheets an application for completing calculations and other logical process on figures (spread out) in rows and columns. For more detail see page 133.

web page a store of information on an Internet (q.v.) server (q.v.) that is available to anyone with access to the Internet.

Web pages invariably have sophisticated facilities; for example, the IPD provides a web page that will enable you to search their library database for a specific book.

what-if models   an application (q.v.) in which a model of a situation is set up – all the components of an employee's remuneration package, for example. In such an example, this model may be used to assess the effect on the organisation's wage bill of changing one or more components in the remuneration package.

The majority of explanations in this glossary is adapted from the British Information Society's glossary (see References below), reprinted by permission of Addison Wesley Longman Ltd.

REFERENCES AND FURTHER READING

THE BRITISH INFORMATION SOCIETY. (1995) *A glossary of computing terms*. 8th ed. London, Addison Wesley Longman.

THE DATA PROTECTION REGISTRAR. *Student information pack*. Available from The Registrar, Wycliffe House, Water Lane, Wilmslow, Cheshire, SK9 5AF.

GALLAGHER M. L. (1991) *Computers and human resource management*. London, Butterworth-Heinemann.

HUMAN RESOURCE MANAGEMENT LTD. (1994) *The HR manager's guide to human resource information systems*. London, Human Resource Information Ltd.

WALKER L. (1993) *Handbook of human resource information systems*. New York, McGraw-Hill.

9 Personal effectiveness

INTRODUCTION

The majority of previous chapters contain sections on the role of the personnel practitioner in, for example, recruitment and selection and in handling disciplinary matters or grievances. You may have been daunted by the multiplicity of roles performed by personnel practitioners. This is not the end of the story, though, because, in order to perform these roles, effective personnel practitioners have to develop some broad skills which have wide-ranging applications. One prime example is interviewing skills. We have seen that personnel practitioners need to possess well-developed interviewing skills for a variety of purposes: selection, discipline and grievance-handling, appraisals, and a whole host of less formal situations.

Interviewing skills having been dealt with in the earlier chapters, in this one we shall be concentrating on the following broad skills areas:

- *communication* – report writing and making presentations
- *counselling* – in handling redundancies, early retirements, sickness absence, and personal problems
- *negotiating, influencing and persuading* – in formal and informal situations
- *time management* – inside and outside the workplace
- *assertiveness* – in work-related and personal situations.

This is not intended to be an exhaustive list, as we are sure that you can think of other useful skills that you use in your jobs as personnel practitioners on a regular basis. Nor are the contents of this chapter intended to provide you with comprehensive reading in these areas. We do hope, however, that you will find this introductory guide a useful starting-point on the road to personal effectiveness in your role as a personnel practitioner, and in life in general. The important topics of self-development and continuing professional development (CPD) are also covered in this chapter (see pages 146–8, 164–5

Undoubtedly you will have already acquired some of the skills listed above owing to your past experiences and innate abilities. Others you will need to work hard at developing by gaining as broad a range of experience as possible. Please note that we are not suggesting that you will ever reach the stage when your skills are honed to such a degree that everything runs smoothly. Life is not like that. In the context of your working life, the organisational environment is in a constant state of change (and, if you think about, without some changes occurring, life would be rather dull). Further, you may find some situations more difficult than others and feel that you will never develop the full range of skills necessary. For instance, part of your job might entail the task of visiting the spouses of employees who have died in service to discuss pension details. The first time that you do this you may feel very inadequate. You will, however, through experience, learn how to effect tasks such as these in a sensitive and professional manner.

WHY IS IT IMPORTANT?

We saw in Chapter 7 that effectiveness means 'doing the right things' (whereas efficiency means 'doing things right'). In the organisational context it has long been recognised that choosing the 'right things to do' at the individual level means performing those activities or attaining those targets that are in line with business or organisational goals. Thus, as personnel practitioners you should seek to determine which activities are the 'right' ones and then acquire the requisite knowledge and skills to perform them to a level that ensures the optimum result. Success then breeds success: a positive result will enhance your status and your credibility in the eyes of your co-workers. That is personal effectiveness.

If you are a member of the IPD, you may find it useful to consult their *Code of professional conduct*, which lays additional responsibilities on you. (At the time of writing the code is being revised.) The IPD code states that:

> Although managing and developing people forms an important part of every manager's job, IPD members can provide specialist professional knowledge, advice and support on the most effective use of human resources. Along with a total commitment to the overall goals of the organisation, they need a detailed understanding of economic, financial, political and social factors so they can play a full role in decision making.

The Code then goes on to define the standards of conduct expected under the headings of Accuracy, Confidentiality, Counselling, Developing Others, Equal Opportunities, Fair Dealing and Self-Development.

Thus, personnel practitioners have a dual role in acquiring the knowledge and skills necessary to perform their tasks and activities effectively at work and to meet the exacting standards laid down by their profession.

Before moving on to look at the skills areas listed above and their importance to you, we shall briefly consider first the much discussed topic of self-development.

SELF-DEVELOPMENT

Torrington and Hall (1991: 474) say that

> to some extent, self-development may be seen as a conscious effort to gain the most from natural learning in a job. The emphasis in self-development is that each individual is responsible for, and can plan, their own development, although they may need to seek help when working on some issues.

So, in aiming to improve your personal effectiveness, you will inevitably have to get involved in some self-development exercises. These should include an initial analysis of your strengths and weaknesses in order to highlight areas that require further development. A plan to concentrate on these development needs can then be put into effect through:

- self-assessment questionnaires

- role-playing 'difficult' situations in a safe environment and carrying out a review of performance, possibly using one or other of the last two points below

- setting up real experiences such as secondments, projects, and work shadowing (see also the section below on increasing your personal profile)

- project work requiring the production of written reports and verbal presentations

- observation and feedback from a trusted third party

- self-analysis of experiences through techniques ranging from diary entries to observation of closed circuit television recordings of real or simulated situations.

In general terms, you will need to experiment with new behaviours and would be advised to follow the simple stages of Kolb's learning cycle in order to gain maximum benefit from the learning experience (see Figure 10).

Figure 10 Kolb's learning cycle

A general point to note is that attempting to improve skills will usually involve a change in behaviour and will often require you to take a risk (of failure). For instance, if you wish to influence the outcome of a particular management decision that is on the agenda of a meeting you are attending then you will not succeed by sitting quietly and taking no part in the discussions. You will, however, have an improved chance of success if, after carrying out some research, you are able to present your findings logically and put forward proposals that are backed up by sound reasoning. This could be done by way of a written report or an oral presentation. Regardless of the outcome, you should then seek honest feedback on your performance from people whose judgement you trust. (We shall see later in the section on Influencing that, at a more advanced level, you may first decide to canvass support from other parties at the meeting to ensure that your ideas get a fair hearing.)

There are two further tips for self-development worthy of comment that will assist you in travelling down the road to enhanced personal effectiveness:

• *Carry out an analysis of how you learn* and make use of this information to plan your learning in the future (Honey and Mumford's 'learning styles questionnaire' is probably the best known in this field – see Chapter 5 and the References section at the end of this chapter).

• *Increase your personal profile* inside and outside your employing organisation by being proactive. At work 'walking the floor' helps you to get to know a large number of employees and, probably more importantly, to become known by them. Also volunteering to take part in activities that extend your normal range of duties, such as taking notes at meetings, involvement in working parties, project work, and making presentations will have the same effect of increasing your profile. If you do not take up such opportunities you may well still be respected for your work, but you will have less chance of really impressing 'onlookers'. Further, a 'backstage worker' approach may mean that someone else gets all the credit for your hard work eg the person whose name ends up on your report, or your boss when he or she presents your proposals to a senior management meeting. Outside work you should set time aside for networking through, for example, getting involved in your local IPD branch activities, and attending seminars, meetings, and other events designed to facilitate networking. You never know: at the next event you could end up sitting alongside your future boss!

Before moving on to enlarge our understanding of the specific skills areas listed above, it is worth bringing to your attention the book by Pedler, Bourgoyne and Boydell (1986). This is excellent, covering a vast number of areas and providing several exercises and questionnaires aimed at an initial self-assessment.

COMMUNICATION

This is a vast subject, so here we shall be concentrating on two main topic areas: one in the field of written communications (ie report writing), and the other (a classic example) in the field of oral communications (ie making presentations). These activities are both important and may often occur together, especially when, as a personnel practitioner, you are engaged in project work. In fact, we should rarely rely on written reports alone if we wish to influence management decisions: the written word may be powerful but oral communications are much more effective here.

Let's take an example of your involvement in issuing an attitude survey to all staff prior to your organisation's being involved in a friendly merger with a former rival. The aim is to gauge the feelings of staff about this change with a view to gradually bringing about some form of culture change in order to ensure as smooth a transition as possible. Your analysis of the attitude survey results and other research evidence would need to be presented in the form of a written report, which would also contain your proposals for the future. Regardless of how well written and presented the report is, it is unlikely to 'sell' itself (after all, you would be dependent on senior managers reading it thoroughly!). Thus it would be advantageous for you to make an oral presentation. This would afford you the opportunity personally to 'sell' your ideas and influence decisions, and will have more impact than the written report on its own. A presentation also lends itself to two-way communication, especially if you incorporate a question-and -answer session to address concerns. Brief guidelines on successful report writing and making presentations are provided below.

Report writing

Reports are written for a variety of reasons. Generally they are documents resulting from research into a particular subject and are intended to convey information and ideas. Reports may lead to action because they help managers to take decisions. There are no rigid rules governing the art of report writing, but there are well-accepted guidelines, summarised below:

A *Terms of reference*. Before you commence any analysis, you must be very clear about your terms of reference:

- *what* is the subject matter of your report (eg sickness absenteeism in Company XYZ)?

- *why* is the report necessary (ie what is its purpose – eg to decrease the level of sickness absence)?

- *who* will read the report and what prior knowledge do they have (eg XYZ's senior management team and a college tutor)?

B *Aim*. You must then determine your overall aim in undertaking this project (eg to decrease the level of sickness absence by 3 to 5 per cent within the next 18 months).

Objectives. The overall aim should then be broken down into specific project objectives, eg:

- to distinguish between the categories of sickness absence (short term *v* long term, casual *v* genuine) in order to calculate the 'size' of the problem

- to compare the levels of each category of sickness absence with those existing within similar organisations or industries

- to analyse the most common reasons for sickness absence and whether these are work-related

- to make proposals to improve the monitoring of sickness absence

- to make proposals to minimise the risk of work-related absences

- to set up a system of sickness absence counselling

- to provide guidelines for managers on the operation of the short-term and long-term sickness absence procedures.

C *Methodology*. Once you know what it is that you are trying to achieve, you can then choose a number of research methods appropriate to the usual constraints of time, money, and accessibility. In our example of sickness absence, suitable methods might include analysis of existing company records, discussions with line managers, questionnaires, comparison with other organisations or industries, and reference to relevant employment legislation and academic texts.

D *Title*. The title page should contain the title, the name of the author, the organisation's name (if appropriate), and the date. Simple as it may sound, the title should be concisely stated and self-explanatory eg 'A review of Sickness Absence in Company XYZ' is not as informative as 'A proposal to decrease the levels of sickness absence within Company XYZ within the next 18 months'.

E *Layout*. Informed opinion is generally in agreement on the following sequence:

- Title page

- Summary (abstract or synopsis)

- Acknowledgements

- Contents page

- Introduction

- Main body

- Conclusions and recommendations

- Appendices

- References and bibliography.

(NB Not all these features need appear in every report.)

F *Check-lists*. Two check-lists are provided in Appendices I and II to give further assistance on the process up to and including the writing up of your report. Like most things, practice makes perfect!

Making presentations

The more inexperienced you are in this area, the more likely you are to be filled with dread at the thought of standing up in front of a group of people to make a formal presentation. There are two main ways of attempting to control your nerves:

- Never do it.

- Take a *risk* and have a go!

If you take the former route, you will never conquer your fear and may impede your career as, more and more, managers and professionals are expected to be able to make effective presentations. If you follow the latter route, you will find that your nervousness will create adrenaline which will help you to perform and that, with good preparation, the use of relaxation techniques, and more experience you will find the fear diminishes. Never expect to become completely laid back at the thought of making a presentation: even very experienced presenters may find the prospect of presenting to an unknown audience a daunting one, but their experience helps them to keep their fears under control.

We obviously recommend that you do 'take a risk' and get into the habit of volunteering to make presentations (sometimes you will be nominated anyway by well-meaning bosses or colleagues). Inevitably you will improve your presentational skills in both formal and informal situations. For instance, you will become more adept at succinctly expressing your point of view in a meeting, even at short notice. You will also increase your profile within the organisation.

We shall now look in more detail at the two stages to making presentations: planning and preparation, and delivery.

Planning and preparation

The approach. You must establish answers to the following questions:

Who?   – the audience   *A*

Why?   – the purpose   *P*

When? – the time   *T*

Where? – the place

What? – the subject

How?   – the means

In a word, your presentation must be *APT*.

The subject matter. There are four stages:

- Do your research.

- Arrange the information logically eg Introduction – Main theme – Summary and Conclusion.

- Prioritise and prune to suit your

  *A*udience

  *P*urpose

  *T*ime.

- Prepare concise notes and visual aids. As for notes, cue cards containing bullet points of information are much easier to use and look more professional than scripts on A4 paper. Further, it is very tempting to read out the latter in full and thus break eye contact with your audience. As for visual aids, each type has advantages and disadvantages – but the bottom line is that they should all be aids and not distractions. They should be *big, bold and simple* to be really effective.

Plan delivery. This will help you to overcome your nervousness.

- Be thoroughly prepared; carry out at least one full dress rehearsal.

- If possible, get feedback on your rehearsal.

- If you know that you tend to get a dry mouth, arrange to have water available.

- If you know that you get a blotchy neck, wear appropriate clothing.

- If you know that your hands tend to shake, don't hold your papers but place them on a table in front of you.

- Adapt the content of your presentation as necessary to ensure that it will be *APT*.

- Practise deep breathing.

Delivery

You will have heard the maxim:

Tell them what you are going to say.   *Introduction*

Say it.   *Main theme*

Then tell them what you have said.   *Conclusion*

Depending on the length of your talk (and it is important to stick to the time allotted, including time for questions and answers), you will be able successfully to present only a limited number of key points. Pick these points carefully and deliver them effectively by:

- being enthusiastic about your subject
- being yourself, with your own style
- speaking naturally, with only minimal reference to notes (if you are well prepared, your cue cards and visual aids will provide the necessary prompts)
- monitoring reactions ie watch out for body language to gauge interest and understanding
- asking questions to keep the audience on their toes.

So how well do you understand delivery? Try answering the following questions. Should you

a) start with an apology because you feel that you are not an expert?

b) start with a joke to lighten the atmosphere if you are inexperienced or do not know your audience?

c) speak quickly in order to get the talk over with?

d) focus on one friendly-looking person to the exclusion of all others?

e) try to copy the style of someone you admire?

f) switch off all the lights and hide behind the overhead projector?

g) not allow time for questions in case you do not know the answers?

h) read straight from comprehensive reference notes to ensure that you do not miss anything out?

i) keep your head down because you are worried that if you look up you will see that everyone is bored (or has left the room)?

j) make extensive use of a whiteboard or flipchart because it provides an opportunity to turn your back on the audience?

k) nail your feet to the floor and not move your hands and arms?

NB In case you had not realised, the answers to all these questions should be NO!

We hope that you find the above guidelines useful in seeking to improve your communication skills, both in report writing and making presentations. Let's now turn to another important communication skill – counselling.

COUNSELLING

The IPD's *Code of professional conduct* (p 6) – currently being updated by the Institute – recognises that personnel practitioners must 'With the relevant skills…be prepared to act as counsellors to individual employees, pensioners and dependants or to refer them, where appropriate, to other professionals or helping agencies'. You should note that counselling *is not* about:

- giving advice

- giving opinions

- sympathising

- giving practical help eg taking over the problem and solving it.

Counselling is not better than these helping devices, but it is different from them and more suited to certain situations. In fact, in one meeting you may need to use a range of helping devices. For instance, when discussing early retirement options with an employee, you will need to:

- counsel the employee to help them decide whether to retire early or not

- give practical help by providing the pensions calculations

- give advice, if requested, about the advantages and disadvantages of a lump sum payment versus an increased annual pension.

Counselling *is* about – in simple terms – *helping people to help themselves*.

Thus a professional counsellor aims to assist 'clients' in exploring their problems, considering the range of options available to them, and deciding on their chosen course of action. Professional counsellors are generally independent third parties with no vested interest in the outcome of the process. As a personnel practitioner this may not be the case, because it is often the actions of the organisation that you represent that have led to the need for counselling. For instance, a potential applicant for early retirement would perhaps not have considered this option if the organisation had not recently announced a major restructuring exercise which may greatly change his or her job role in the future. Thus the personnel practitioner should aim to counsel the 'client' following the tips described below, though inevitably with one eye on the organisational circumstances ie the need to equip the organisation with new skills to meet future market needs.

Counselling is a complex subject, as is evident from the number of professionally trained specialists in the field. As a personnel practitioner, you will increasingly find that managers and employees expect you to be the person responsible for dealing with those problems that require counselling as the helping style. We do not wish to suggest that, after a little practice, you would be competent in dealing with every possible situation requiring counselling skills in the workplace. As the saying goes, a little knowledge can be a dangerous thing. You should seek to develop your counselling skills so that you are able to help some employees in some situations, even if it is only in a very limited way. If you have a tendency to try to avoid dealing with employees who you know have particular problems, you will be seen as an unapproachable and uncaring employer. You may even lose good employees because you did not take the appropriate action at the time.

One story worth relating is that of a young brother and sister who lost their father. Both went straight back to work on the day after the funeral, but each had rather different experiences. On her return to work, the sister was invited into the office of the personnel officer, who expressed his sympathy (he had previously sent a note signed by the young woman's colleagues together with flowers from the company) and reassured her that if she felt she could not cope with coming back to work so soon, she should just inform him and he would make the appropriate arrangements with her manager. On the other hand, when the woman's brother returned to work, nothing was said by his supervisor at all, though he had known why the young man had been absent. In fact, a couple of days later, when he was feeling very disheartened, his supervisor said to him in the hearing of other workers, 'It's about time you pulled yourself together.' Can you guess which employee remained longer with their employer?

Unfortunately, employees seem to suffer from a vast range of problems eg drugs, drink, bereavement, debt, AIDS, physical or mental ill health, and troublesome relationships (to name but a few). If you are faced with an approach – usually prefaced by 'Have you got a minute to spare?' – from an employee, then, when they are unburdening their souls to you (and taking considerably more than a minute to do so), remember this safeguard: *know your limitations*. In other words, if you feel out of your depth, you should acknowledge this and help the employee by referring them to a specialist for advice.

There are, however, a number of commonly occurring situations that you will be expected to deal with personally. These include redundancy, early retirement, sickness absence, work-related problems, and some personal problems. In fact, organisations often have in place formalised counselling procedures to deal with such situations (such as the one detailed in Chapter 6, page 95). In such cases the counselling procedure replaces, or runs in parallel with, other procedures. (See the ACAS publications *Discipline at work* (section 4) and *Redundancy handling* for further details.)

It is not our intention to provide a comprehensive guide to suit every occasion, but a few simple tips are offered below. These should be read and implemented in the context of each situation that you deal with and in accordance with the appropriate organisational procedures.

Tips
- Listen actively.

- Show empathy ie non-critical, non-judgmental acceptance.

- Reflect back and paraphrase what has been said.

- Use open questioning.

- Ask questions to ensure that the client focuses on the problem.

- Prompt (but do not direct) exploration of a range of options.

- Provide summaries throughout of what has been said or agreed.

- Encourage the client to find his or her own solution and set his or her own goals.

- Agree an action plan.

- Summarise at the end.

- Monitor and review (if appropriate ie if you are dealing with work-related issues).

A word of caution here. Don't expect too much from a 30- to 60-minute counselling session. Counselling takes time, because clients are often trying to work through complex problems. Don't, though, be tempted simply to allocate a larger chunk of time on the next occasion, because short sessions with 'thinking time' in between are usually more fruitful. If you have practised good counselling skills, your client can leave the meeting better equipped to think through the options before reaching a decision on what to do next. He or she may decide not to *do* anything but, as a result of the counselling, may feel better equipped to deal with the situation than before.

We shall now consider the skills of negotiating, influencing, and persuading.

NEGOTIATING, INFLUENCING, AND PERSUADING

As a personnel practitioner, you are likely to find yourself in situations, formal and informal, that require you to use negotiating skills in order to reach an agreement. Further, you will find it difficult to promote your ideas, affect decisions, and 'sell' changes without well-developed influencing skills. Both of these need to be backed up by powerful persuasion techniques and assertive behaviour (the latter subject will be discussed in a separate section later in this chapter).

There are several definitions of negotiation, but we shall use that provided by Alan Fowler (1995: 1)

> Negotiation occurs whenever there is an issue that cannot be resolved by one person acting alone; it occurs when the two (or more) people who have to be involved begin with different views on how to proceed, or have different aims for the outcome.

Negotiations do not have to result in win/lose outcomes but may lead to win/win results. For example, if I have an orange that you and I both want, and we negotiate, there are various possible outcomes:

- I keep the orange.   – *I win, you lose*

- You get the orange.   – *You win, I lose*

- We cut the orange in half.   – *I win, you win (compromise)*

- We divide the orange so that   – *I win, you win (collaboration)*
  I keep the peel for baking a cake
  and you get the fruit to decorate
  a drink.

Fowler (1995: 2) also provides us with definitions of influence and persuasion:

> Influence is a broad concept, involving the effect on each person of the whole context in which the discussion takes place, including the quality of past and present working relationships as well as each participant's unspoken ambitions or fears. Persuasion involves all those skills of argument and discussion that can be used by one person to obtain another's agreement.

Thus, as personnel practitioners, you will frequently be in situations, ranging from formal meetings to chance corridor discussions with other parties, when you will need to use influence and persuasion to reach an agreed outcome. For instance, we mentioned in Chapter 6 that sometimes there is no satisfactory resolution to a grievance. In such cases you will need to persuade the employee(s) concerned to accept that there is no point in continuing to pursue their grievance to the next stage, because the answer there will be the same. You would be advised to prepare yourself by considering the influencing factors listed below and the skills of persuasion outlined in Table 11 on page 158.

Fowler describes the range of influencing factors that are used in such circumstances and points out that:

- you should be aware of them so that you are not unduly influenced by them

- you should use them to your own advantage when they apply in your favour.

You should therefore compare yourself with the other party in a negotiating situation by examining the following influencing factors:

- the personal relationship ie past history

- any status differences

- connections with sources of organisational power

- the formality of the location and the negotiating situation (and whose style this suits best)

- the level of information and experience

- gender, race, and age differences

- reputations – for success or failure

- expectations about outcomes

- timing – duration and deadlines

- work pressures.

Once you have carried out this analysis, you can use some of these factors to your advantage and resist the temptation to be adversely influenced by those that favour the other party – or you may positively take action to counter them. Let's consider a particular scenario in order to demonstrate this last point.

Under the earlier section in this chapter on self-development we considered a situation in which you might wish to influence the outcome of a management decision under discussion at a meeting. Let's assume that the topic for discussion is the reduction of car parking spaces due to the erection of a Portakabin for contract workers. The car park is used by technical and office workers during the day and shopfloor workers at night (and a small number of technical staff who work nights on a rotational basis). The meeting is a staff consultative committee, and you represent the technical department at that meeting. You have seen that this item is on the agenda circulated prior to the meeting, and are concerned at the effect that it would have. There is already pressure for spaces at night time because the shift for the technical staff commences after that of the shopfloor workers. Your informal analysis shows that 90 per cent of the technical staff bring their own cars to work, and all would have concerns for their safety and that of their cars if they had to park further away from the main building at night time. You decide on two possible solutions: to designate three spaces for the use of the technical staff at night time (but you are not confident that this will be adhered to), or to relocate the Portakabin.

You know that the chairperson will normally introduce such a measure as a *fait accompli*, and you realise that there are several influencing factors that act in his favour: he is senior in status to you and has more influence with important members of senior management. Further, he is known to be fairly dogmatic in outlook, but is also under a lot of work pressure at present.

So, in this scenario you have carried out your research, considered alternatives, and can put forward proposals, backed up by sound reasoning. You also decide to take the earlier piece of advice and canvass support from one of the engineers present at the meeting (thereby discovering that the engineers' 'on call' system will provide them with similar problems). You successfully gain some 'air time', and the *pièce de résistance*, from the chairperson's point of view, is that you then offer – on the condition that the committee accepts your proposal – to talk to the chief engineer and health and safety officer to decide on an alternative location for the Portakabin. The chairperson may be known to be dogmatic but, faced with sound reasoning and someone prepared to take responsibility for the problem, he is likely now to be much less inclined to make the influencing factors work in his favour. You, on the other hand, have not only resisted the urge to be daunted by those factors but have found a way of working around them!

Let's now consider your powers of persuasion. Fowler (1995: 31) provides an excellent self-assessment questionnaire to investigate this. Analyse the range of negotiating situations that you are currently involved in before responding honestly to the statements in Table 11. Think of situations that are formal and informal, and that take place inside and outside the workplace.

Obviously you are aiming to develop your powers of persuasion so that you will eventually be able to award yourself a rating of 5 on each criteria; to be realistic, this may never happen, but in the meantime the results will show which areas you should start working on.

We have now looked at the three areas: negotiating, influencing, and persuading, and have seen how interlinked they are. Another important and connected behavioural style is assertion, but before we deal with this, we shall take time to look at the techniques of good time management.

Table 11 Assess your powers of persuasion

	Rarely 1	2	3	4	Always 5
1 I adopt a positive and collaborative style.					
2 I am successful in avoiding confrontation.					
3 I assess the other person's viewpoint.					
4 I adapt my position to reflect the other person's viewpoint.					
5 I encourage a dialogue and do not set out all my case immediately.					
6 I do not interrupt the other person when they make statements I disagree with.					
7 I am a very attentive listener.					
8 I use questions, not statements, to probe or challenge the other person's case.					
9 If I need time for thought, or for emotions to cool, I seek an adjournment.					
10 I first introduce proposals for compromise or concession on a no-commitment basis.					
11 I link my proposed concessions to moves by the other person.					
12 I emphasise the benefits to the other person of proposed compromise.					
13 I use summaries to ensure mutual understanding and move the discussion on.					
14 I take the initiative in bringing the discussion to a constructive close.					
15 I ensure any agreement includes details of how it will be implemented.					
16 I ensure any agreement is mutually understood and is not ambiguous.					
17 I observe body language for clues about attitudes and intentions.					

The header reads: Rate yourself on a scale of 1 to 5

TIME MANAGEMENT

Like all busy managers, personnel practitioners are likely to find that there appears to be a serious mismatch between their volume of work and the time they have to do it in. This is especially so when a large part of each day seems to be taken up with dealing with queries from employees and other parties. A lot of people attend courses in order to learn about good time management techniques. They often get very enthusiastic about how they will revolutionise their working (and personal) life by employing these techniques at the conclusion of the training course. The problem is that when they get back to the workplace, nothing (and no one) else has changed, so they find that they lack the time to try out any new ideas or to develop the necessary skills. In fact, 'it takes time to save time' initially because good time management involves more planning and preparation; it is often easier to slip back into old habits and react to emergencies and crises rather than thinking ahead to try to avoid them.

It is also difficult to initiate the application of good time management skills at home because if this involves persuading other family members to take more responsibility for, say, certain household chores then they may be inclined to be uncooperative, as the benefits to them are not immediately apparent. Here we can see the link between the previous section on negotiating, influencing, and persuading and good time management, as well as a link with the following section on assertiveness. It is necessary to use and develop all these skills if you really want to change your time management habits.

As we have already said, developing skills usually means changing behaviour. With time management in particular you are attempting to change patterns of behaviour that have been ingrained over many years, so don't expect a miracle cure. The good news is that once you begin the process and start to see the benefits, you will be greatly encouraged to carry on. The new patterns of behaviour in the workplace will start to spill over into your personal life as you gain the confidence to try to change others' behaviour along with your own.

First, let's examine some fallacies about time management.

Table 12 Time management

Fallacies	The truth
Time management will mean that I have to work efficiently all the time.	Time management *will* help you to work efficiently, but only when you want to. You may choose to work efficiently for just some of the time – for example, on priority tasks.
Time management will mean that I'll be so busy that I'll miss out on things like gossiping with colleagues or taking my time over a favourite job.	Time management helps you to choose the right things to do and to work through them more quickly. You will then free up extra time and you can decide how to spend it.
Time management will mean that I can no longer be spontaneous eg agree to help out a colleague or accept an invitation from a friend.	Time management will help you to avoid crisis management but should not remove spontaneity. You can choose which aspects of your life you wish to retain.
Time management will mean that I have to work a lot harder overall.	Time management should mean that you do less work overall because you will decide which tasks are the important ones ie the ones that contribute most to your goals. **You will work smarter, not harder.**

A fundamental stage in time management is to decide on our goals and priorities and then choose to work on tasks that help us to achieve them. Those tasks that do not fall into this category will then either come lower down our list of priorities or will cease to be performed at all. In discussing time management we are referring to the distinction between efficiency and effectiveness: *efficiency is doing things right, effectiveness is doing the right things*.

These memorable definitions help us to remember that we should always aim to be effective rather than efficient. Many people pride themselves on being efficient, but that may mean that they are simply working hard to achieve tasks rather than working towards goals. Thus they may be wasting a lot of their time and will probably see other (more effective) people being promoted over them.

Good time management results in

- more productivity

- more control

- more time for leisure

- less stress

- more effective decision-making

- success.

We shall now consider the most common time-wasters for personnel practitioners and suggest some time management techniques for you to try out – see Table 13 (on page 161). Some of our suggestions assume that you have responsibilities for staff (and can therefore delegate some tasks). We have suggested alternative techniques where this is not the case. Remember that you will need to take time out initially to decide on your goals and priorities and to plan how you will achieve them. Don't try to implement everything at once: practise one or two new techniques at a time to see which ones work for you.

We have covered this important skill very quickly. Now you need to take *time* to do some further reading around this subject, making use of self-assessment questionnaires to determine your strengths and weaknesses in this area. Plan next to do something specific in order to improve your time management. It can be done: many others have been successful before you.

We shall leave this section with the following five steps to developing good time management habits:

1 *Recognise* the difficulty in changing.

2 *Develop* a better way.

3 *Launch* the new habit strongly.

4 *Practise* the new way often.

5 Allow *no exceptions*.

ASSERTIVENESS

Assertiveness is probably the most useful skill of all. Developing it will have an immediate impact on your working and non-working life. Assertiveness is clear, honest, and direct communication which pays heed to our own needs and the needs of others. It is best described by comparing it to the two extremes of submissive and aggressive styles of behaviour; see Tables 14 and 15 (both adapted from Back K. and K. (1986)).

Table 13 How to avoid time-wasters

Time-wasters	Techniques
Interruptions (telephone calls, drop-in visitors)	• Operate a limited 'open door' policy. • Remove yourself to work undisturbed elsewhere. • Stand up when answering the telephone; tell the caller that you will call him or her back at a mutually convenient time. • Get someone to screen your calls and callers – either an assistant or a colleague (in the latter case you could set up a reciprocal and mutually convenient arrangement to cater for periods of intense pressure from work deadlines).
Poorly conducted meetings	• Have a personal agenda covering what you want to achieve during the meeting and work towards it. • Be assertive and suggest time limits for each item. • Gather support to suggest changes to the meeting eg limited duration, less frequent, more informative/participative.
Too much paperwork	• Keep a tidy desk and tackle one task at a time (do not 'grass-hop' between different tasks). • Speed-read; you won't need to remember every detail of the communication – just the gist of it. • Adopt a simple filing system and stick to it. • Thin files out periodically to save time when referring to them. • Handle pieces of paper once only using the RAFT* system. • When possible, reply with short notes/memos/telephone calls rather than long-winded responses.
Poor delegation	• Delegate finite or routine tasks. • Ask for regular status reports. • Resist the temptation to get involved in the minute detail of a task.
Reverse delegation (when staff offload their tasks onto the boss)	• Listen to the problem but resist the urge to take it over. • Insist that staff present problems *and* some suggestions to solve them. • Support your staff in making *their* decisions.
Poor work-scheduling	• Use an 'organiser' to list your 'to do' tasks, and keep this up to date. • Set your own deadlines and priorities and stick to them; whenever feasible, don't allow other people's priorities to override your own. • Always allow for some undisturbed time during the day, and use this for thinking time or work on major projects (preferably when your energy levels are at their optimum).
Perfectionism	• Attention to detail has its place but don't allow this to get in the way of achieving the task. • Allow yourself to produce the standard of work that is appropriate to the circumstances (and helps you to achieve your goals).
Poor use of technology	• Get up to speed with time-saving technology eg word processing, spreadsheets, database packages. • Use telephone memories/answering facilities/divert systems.
Lack of leisure time	• Schedule in leisure time/treats to your day. • Resist the temptation to use your leisure time to meet other needs eg to complete a large project. • Keep fit: a healthy body helps you to perform better mentally.

*RAFT: *R*efer it   *A*ct on it   *F*ile it   *T*hrow it away

Table 14 Behaviour styles

Assertive	Submissive	Aggressive
Communicates impression of self-respect and respect for others.	Communicates a message of inferiority and results in lowered self-esteem.	Communicates impression of superiority and disrespect
Our wants, needs, and rights are viewed as equal to those of others.	Allows the wants, needs, and rights of others to be more important than own.	Puts own wants, needs, and rights above those of other people.
Achieves own objectives by influencing, listening, and negotiating. Others are able to co-operate willingly.	Ignores own rights and needs in an attempt to satisfy the needs of other people.	Achieves own objectives by not allowing others a choice. Violates the rights of others.
Behaviour is active, direct and honest.	Anger towards others is directed inwards.	Behaviour is domineering, self-centred, and self-enhancing.
I'm OK...You're OK	*I'm not OK...You are*	*I'm OK...You're not*

Table 15 What are the differences?

Assertive	Submissive	Aggressive
Verbal		
'I' statements that make it clear you are speaking for yourself eg 'I think', 'I would like', 'I feel.'	Few 'I' statements, and those often qualified eg 'It's only my idea but...'.	'I' statements that are boastful or too numerous, and the use of the royal 'we' when it is really 'I' eg 'We don't want to do that.'
Distinctions made between fact and opinion eg 'As I see it...', 'My opinion is...'.	Opinions qualified with such words as 'maybe', 'perhaps', 'I wonder', 'possibly'.	Opinions expressed as facts eg 'The scheme's crazy.'
Statements or questions that acknowledge disagreement and seek to resolve it eg 'We have a disagreement on this, so how can we move it forward?'	Statements that downplay a disagreement or pretend that it does not exist eg 'Well, having aired that one, I think it's best if we move on.'	Statements that inflame or keep disagreements going eg 'Anybody with an ounce of common sense can see that won't work!'
Voice		
Tone – steady, firm, clear.	Tone – apologetic, wobbly, dull, monotonous.	Tone – harsh, sarcastic, blaming, challenging.
Volume – not overloud or quiet; may be raised to get attention.	Volume – quiet, dropping away at the end.	Volume – overloud, rising at the end.
Body language		
Gestures – open hand movements used with firm, measured pace to emphasise or demonstrate. Arms open or lightly crossed.	Gestures – covering mouth with hand, tight and nervous hand movements, eg fiddling with pen.	Gestures – dismissive hand movements, pointing with finger/pen, thumping table, 'steepling' (ie finger tips pressed together as sign of superiority), arms crossed high (ie unapproachable).
Posture – upright but relaxed, moving slightly forward.	Posture – shoulders hunched, huddled over papers.	Posture – head in air, chin thrust out, leaning far back, hands behind head.
Eyes – direct, relaxed gaze.	Eyes – averted.	Eyes – glaring, hostile.

Now that you are familiar with the differences between these three behavioural styles, you should note the following three essential skills of assertive behaviour, summarised by Anne Dickson (1985: 22) as follows:

1 Decide what it is you want or feel, and say so specifically and directly.

2 Stick to your statement, repeating it, if necessary, over and over again. (This is commonly known as the Broken Record Approach).

3 Assertively deflect any responses from the other person which might undermine your assertive stance, ie acknowledge the response but do not allow yourself to become side-tracked or involved in an argument eg 'I know that you're tired as well but I still want you to help with the housework'; 'I know that you're disappointed but I still have to say 'no'.'

We can see in Table 15 that assertive behaviour involves lots of 'I' statements. It also involves the use of the word 'no', which can be a very difficult lesson for us to learn. If, for instance, a colleague asks you to help out with some salary calculations so that she can meet a deadline for a report on anticipated labour costs, your first inclination is likely to be to agree. This is acceptable so long as:

• your own work does not suffer

• you know that your colleague will be glad to return the favour at a later date

• you do not feel that your colleague is taking advantage of your better nature (and is only in this predicament through her own fault).

However, if any of these preconditions do not exist, then you should seriously consider saying no. Remember that by saying no *you are refusing the request, not rejecting the person.* You will find that if you say no assertively the person concerned will not consider that you have let him or her down or hurt his or her feelings. It will instead be clear that you simply cannot help him or her to solve this particular problem. So, in appropriate circumstances, practise saying no *clearly and definitely* without excessive apology or excuses and *directly* without lying or letting the other person down.

As a personnel practitioner, you will be dealing with all sorts of people in a variety of emotional states eg upset, nervous, under pressure, angry, dogmatic, inconsiderate. There will be occasions when you feel that submissive or aggressive behaviour is more appropriate than assertive behaviour. An example of the former situation might be when you are not as interested in the outcome of a discussion as the other party and so allow their views to override your own. An example of the latter might be when you use aggression in a controlled way to indicate that you really have come to the end of the road in a negotiating situation.

The choice of behavioural styles is always open to you. However, by practising assertive behaviour you are ensuring that you do consciously choose a particular style rather than rely on that behavioural style which is your natural tendency.

SUMMARY

In this chapter we have looked at a range of topics pertinent to your role as a personnel practitioner. We have not tried to provide a comprehensive coverage, either in range or content, but an introductory guide to a number of skills areas. As your career progresses, you will find development of these skills is invaluable in helping you to perform difficult tasks and activities in as professional a manner as possible.

The skills and techniques of report writing and making presentations were chosen as prime examples of communication skills that help you to 'sell' your ideas and proposals. The counselling skills necessary to deal with the vast range of problems that are likely to face members of your workforce were dealt with next. The connected skills of negotiating, influencing, and persuading and their application in both formal and informal situations were also considered, as was the vexing problem of managing your time. If you cannot manage yourself, it may be difficult to convince others that you are worthy of promotion, when you will also be managing others.

Finally, we proposed that assertive behaviour is appropriate in nearly every role played by the personnel practitioner in the workplace (and in many other situations occurring outside it, too). It is an important skill which backs up the others necessary for you to achieve personal effectiveness. We ended with assertion because, of all the skills areas we have considered in this chapter, you cannot afford to ignore this one. Assertive behaviour is enormously powerful and, used correctly, helps to build your credibility in the workplace. Try it at work and at home – you'll be amazed by the results.

CONCLUSION

Two terms are commonly used when discussing personal effectiveness: they are continuous development and, increasingly, continuing professional development (CPD). The first term basically means learning from real experiences at work on a continuous basis eg not assuming that a two-day skills training programme will provide delegates with all they need to become fully competent in the skill concerned. Thus learning continues throughout our working lives through formal events such as training programmes, but also through our day-to-day experiences, planned and unplanned.

The second and connected term is increasingly being adopted by professional bodies such as the IPD to reassure outside parties that members of the Institute are fully competent in today's working environment ie that they did not put all their books and journals away on qualifying but take great pains to keep up to date with legislation and other developments in the field of personnel management. Thus CPD is a requirement for Corporate Member status of the IPD, and evidence will be required at the time of upgrading membership and on a random selection basis at any time. Records should show a mix of learning activities, such as those that are work-based, courses, seminars, conferences, and self-directed or informal learning, as well as a synopsis of how the learning has been used or will be used in future activities (eg summarising the outcome after reading a journal article).

The IPD Policy on CPD states five essential principles:

- Development should be continuous in the sense that the professional should always be actively seeking improved performance.

- Development should be owned and managed by the individual learner.

- CPD is a personal matter and the effective learner knows best what he or she needs to learn. Development should begin from the individual's current learning state.

- Learning objectives should be clear and wherever possible should serve organisational or client needs as well as individual goals.

- Regular investment of time in learning should be seen as an essential part of professional life, not as an optional extra.

The main message here is that the acquisition of skills is not a finite exercise. We can never be fully effective in all situations and are constantly thrown into new experiences which promote new learning. This chapter can provide only a brief introduction to some of the skills necessary for increased personal effectiveness in your role as a personnel practitioner. Completion of a number of appropriate activities, referred to in the next section, will provide you with a useful starting-point before you undertake some further reading into those skill areas that you decide are priorities for you. A number of recommended video titles are also included at the end of this chapter (you will find these particularly useful if visual messages are more appropriate to your learning style). *You should aim continuously to develop yourself throughout your working life.*

We wish you every success!

ACTIVITIES

1 If you are a member of the IPD, obtain the IPD's pack on CPD. Use it to set up a record of your CPD and a development plan. Discuss your development plan with one or more of your learning sources in order to gain their support in putting some of your action plans into effect.

2 Pick a personnel issue that is topical within your organisation and carry out some research by studying information available internally, eg statistical data, minutes of meetings, and externally, eg legislation, journal articles. Write a short report to an appropriate member of management. In your report, examine the issue and put forward proposals as to how the organisation should respond. Follow the guidelines provided in this chapter on effective report writing.

3 Volunteer to make a presentation to an outside body (eg a local school) on, say, the work of a personnel practitioner or on your organisation as an attractive employer. Follow the guidelines provided in this chapter.

4 Buy a book on one of the topics covered in this chapter eg negotiating, time management, or assertiveness. Apply the techniques that you learn about to any important situation that you are currently facing. Use any self-assessment exercises and questionnaires provided in the book to begin the process of increasing your self-awareness. (Recommended titles are detailed in the further reading listed below.)

APPENDIX I TO CHAPTER 9

Check-list: the mechanics of report writing

Terms of reference	• Are you clear about the purpose of your report?
	• Have you specified the aim and objectives?
	• Are you clear about who will read your report and their level of knowledge?
Collecting information	• Have you used a workable recording system?
	• Have you collected information from as many sources as possible?
Organising information	• Is your report presented in clear sections?
	• Are they logically sequenced and easy to follow?
	• Do you provide signposts for the reader?
Grammar and style	• Are your paragraphs short, clearly defined in material, and easy to read?
	• Have you chosen simple, unambiguous wording?
	• Have you checked sentence construction, spelling, and punctuation?
	• Is the style appropriate to the content of the report, your organisation, and the reader(s)?
Checking your work	• Have you checked structure and language?
	• Have you asked for a third person's comments?
	• Have you proofread your final draft?
Layout	• Have you presented your report in the accepted organisational format?
	• Are the sections numbered and headings highlighted consistently?
	• Are quotes/illustrations/appendices/cross-references all referred to correctly?
Final presentation	• Have you given the typist clear instructions?
	• Have you chosen the most suitable form of presentation and distribution?
	• Have you allowed enough time for these final stages?

APPENDIX II TO CHAPTER 9

Check-list: The layout/contents of your report

Title page	• Does the report have a short, self-explanatory title?
	• Does the title page contain other appropriate identification data eg name of organisation, name of author, date of completion?
Summary	• Does it give the reader a framework showing the main features of each section?
	• Does it include any conclusions reached?
	• Is it self-contained and self-explanatory?
Acknowledgements	• Do they record a debt for help or use of facilities?
Contents page	• Are section/page numbers clear and accurate?
Introduction	• Does it refer to the terms of reference, limitations or constraints, scope, and the research method(s) you have adopted?
	• Does it contain appropriate background information (depending on the needs of the reader(s))?
Body of the report	• Do you provide an analysis of the perceived problem and include the research findings?
	• Does the discussion lead naturally on to the conclusions and recommendations of the report?
Conclusions	• Do you summarise your main research findings?
	• Do you state clearly your interpretation of these results?
Recommendations	• Have you considered a number of alternatives before deciding on your recommendations?
	• Have you written clear recommendations which are well-reasoned and costed and which include time-scales?
Appendices	• Do they contain lengthy or technical information?
	• Are they correctly referenced in the report?
References	• Has a consistent referencing system been used?
	• Have you included full details: surname, initials, title of article/book/journal, date of publication, volume/issue/page numbers?
Bibliography	• Do you acknowledge other works used and those for useful further reading?

REFERENCES AND FURTHER READING

The following are available from the Advisory, Conciliation and Arbitration Service (ACAS), ACAS Reader Ltd, P.O. Box 16, Earl Shilton, Leicester, LE9 8ZZ; tel. 01455 852 225:

Advisory booklet on redundancy handling. (Undated) Leicester, ACAS.

Advisory handbook on discipline at work. (Amended 1989) Leicester, ACAS.

BACK K. *and* K. (1986) 'Assertiveness training for meetings'. *Industrial and Commercial Training.* Vol. 18, No. 2, March/April. pp26–30.

BENNETT R. (1994) *Personal effectiveness.* London, Kogan Page.

BLANCHARD K. *et al.* (1990) *The one minute manager meets the monkey.* London, Fontana.

COVEY S. (1994) *First things first.* London, Simon & Schuster.

The following is available from Croner Publications Ltd, Croner House, London Road, Kingston-upon-Thames, Surrey, KT2 6SR; tel. 0181 547 3465:

Croner's personnel assistant's handbook. Kingston-upon-Thames, Surrey. (The Skills section covers presentation skills, conducting disciplinary and grievance interviews, performance appraisal, counselling absentees, time management, and report writing.)

DICKSON A. (1984) *A woman in your own right: assertiveness and you.* London, Quartet Books.

FOWLER A. (1995) *Negotiating, persuading and influencing.* London, Institute of Personnel and Development.

FRITCHIE R. *and* Melling M. (1991) *The business of assertiveness: a practical guide to being more effective in the workplace.* London, BBC Books.

GILLEN T. (1997) *Assertiveness.* London, Institute of Personnel and Development.

GILLEN T. (1995) *Positive influencing skills.* London, Institute of Personnel and Development.

HONEY P. *and* MUMFORD A. (1986) *The manual of learning styles.* Maidenhead, Peter Honey.

INSTITUTE OF PERSONNEL AND DEVELOPMENT. (1997) *IPD guide on counselling.* London, Institute of Personnel and Development.

INSTITUTE OF PERSONNEL AND DEVELOPMENT. (1997) *IPD guide on redundancy.* London, Institute of Personnel and Development.

INSTITUTE OF PERSONNEL AND DEVELOPMENT. (Undated) *IPD code of professional conduct.* London, Institute of Personnel and Development.

INSTITUTE OF PERSONNEL AND DEVELOPMENT. (Undated) *IPM statement on continuous development.* London, Institute of Personnel and Development.

JAY A. (1990) *Effective presentation: the communication of ideas by words and visual aids.* B.I.M.

KOLB D. A. *et al.* (1974) *Organisational psychology: an experiential approach.* Hemel Hempstead, Prentice Hall.

LEIGH A. (1997) *Persuasive reports and proposals.* London, Institute of Personnel and Development.

MACDONALD J. W. (1992) *Report writing.* London, Croner Publications Ltd.

MAITLAND I. (1995) *Managing your time.* London, Institute of Personnel and Development.

MEGRANAHAN M. (1989) *Counselling: a practical guide for employers.* London, Institute of Personnel Management.

PEDLER M., BOURGOYNE J. *and* BOYDELL T. (1986) *A manager's guide to self development.* London, McGraw-Hill.

SUMMERFIELD J. *and* VAN OUDTSHOORN L. (1995) *Counselling in the workplace.* London, Institute of Personnel and Development.

TORRINGTON D. *and* HALL L. (1991) *Personnel management: a new approach.* Hemel Hempstead, Prentice Hall.

VIDEOS

Can you spare a moment? (1987) Video Arts (counselling).

I wasn't prepared for that. (1996) Video Arts (making presentations).

Negotiating: tying the knot. (1996) Video Arts.

The unorganised manager. (1996) Video Arts (time management).

Report writing. (1993) Video Arts.

Straight talking. (1993) Video Arts (assertiveness).

Index

The People and Organisations Series

PROFESSIONAL QUALIFICATIONS

This series has been commissioned specially for students setting out on a professional career in personnel and development.

The Institute of Personnel and Development's new professional qualification scheme came into effect in July 1996. It comprises three parts:

• core management

• core personnel and development

• any four from a range of more than 20 generalist and specialist electives.

The series starts by addressing core personnel and development and four generalist electives: employee reward, employee resourcing, employee relations, and employee development. Together, these cover the personnel and development knowledge requirements for graduateship of the IPD (or their N/SVQ Level 4 equivalents).

INFORMATIVE AND COMPETENCY-BASED

Each of these core texts follows the syllabus closely and should constitute students' main source of ideas, information, and guidance. The emphasis is as much on skills development as on theory, so students will gain a firm foundation for applying and using their knowledge in a variety of situations. The books include mini-cases and examples drawn from a wide spectrum of organisations and employment contexts.

AUTHORITATIVE

Each book is written by the chief examiner in the relevant area, follows the syllabus closely and provides essential reading not just for students taking the IPD Professional Qualification Scheme but for all those undertaking courses with a human resource management component.

SERIES EDITORS

Mick Marchington is professor of human resource management at the Manchester School of Management, UMIST, where he has worked since the mid-1980s. He is currently chief examiner for Core Personnel and Development and has played a major part in the redesign of the Professional Qualification Scheme. He has written widely elsewhere on employee relations and human resource management, specialising in the areas of employee involvement, workplace industrial relations, human resource management in retailing and, more recently, on the links between human resource management and total quality management. He wrote the chapter on employee relations in *Strategic prospects for HRM* (1995, IPD) and also contributed to the IPD's research report on *Quality*.

Mike Oram is a human resource professional whose career has also spanned general management, information systems, legal affairs, and academia. He has for many years been at the forefront as group personnel manager and company secretary with the Prestcold Group and as director of personnel and corporate affairs with Toshiba (UK) Ltd. He is co-author of *Re-engineering's missing ingredient: the human factor* (1995, IPD) and is also a fellow of the IPD. As the IPD's vice-president for Membership and Education he has been closely involved in discussions leading up to the new qualification scheme.

Employee Development

Rosemary Harrison

Building on the success of her best-selling book, *Employee development* (1992, IPD), in the IPD's Management Studies Series, Rosemary Harrison has created a completely new text to take full account of the changes in the new syllabus requirements and the wider training scene.

The book is divided into four parts and covers the following areas:

- employee development and the business
- the context for employee development
  - national and international context
  - organisational and professional context
- developing the corporate curriculum
- promoting organisational learning and advancement.

Rosemary Harrison is a graduate of Kings College, London University. Since 1989 she has been lecturer in human resource management at Durham University Business School where she is also director of its human resource development unit. She has worked as a consultant in many British private- and public-sector organisations and has written several books on human resource management and development. She has recently been appointed chief examiner in employee development for the IPD's new Professional Standards.

June 1997 480 pages Paperback ISBN 0 85292 657 X **£19.95**

Employee Relations
John Gennard and Graham Judge

To help prospective personnel managers develop the necessary skills, the authors have taken a wholly pragmatic managerial perspective. The book is written to the syllabus requirements and combines theory with practice to enable all students to apply their knowledge and understanding in unfamiliar or difficult situations.

Each chapter contains exercises, mini case-studies, and examples of real-life situations from all sectors of industry, commerce, and public authorities.

The book is divided into two parts and covers:

• employee relations organisations

• employee processes

• outcomes of employee relations

• employee relations management and the corporate environment

• negotiation skills – general overview

• handling grievances

• handling disciplinary matters

• bargaining

• devising, implementing and monitoring schedules

• evaluating new employee relations management.

John Gennard is professor of human resource management at Strathclyde Business School. He is also the IPD's chief examiner for employee relations.

June 1997 288 pages Paperback ISBN 0 85292 654 5 **£19.95**

Employee Resourcing

Ted Johns and Stephen Taylor

This comprehensive book examines global influences on British decision-making and the transformations we are now witnessing within the nature of work and jobs. It makes clear that many of the traditional techniques of employee resourcing require radical rethinking.

The book considers in detail all the key processes:

- forecasting internal movement and external labour supply

- organising systematic recruitment campaigns: job analysis, person specification, and focused search techniques

- selecting the right candidate through interviews, psychometric tests, and assessment centres

- defining, monitoring, and managing performance

- designing performance review systems and creating guidelines for appraisal meetings

- monitoring and controlling attendance

- designing, implementing, and reviewing retirement and redundancy programmes

- establishing an ethical framework for justified dismissals.

Ted Johns is an independent management consultant specialising in the improvement of organisational performance. He is chief examiner for the Employee Resourcing module as well as an examiner for the Institute of Chartered Secretaries and Administrators, and the Chartered Institute of Marketing. He is, with Stephen Connock, co-author of *Ethical leadership* (IPD, 1995).

January 1998 288 pages (approx.) Paperback ISBN 0 85292 624 3 **£19.95**

Employee Reward
Michael Armstrong

Reward is one of the central creative accountabilities for all personnel professionals. When used effectively as a strategic tool, it can play a key role in communicating values, promoting flexibility, and maximising individual contributions to organisational objectives. This book sets out the central competences that all practitioners need in their portfolio.

Decisions about pay are inevitably influenced by local labour markets, the wider national and international context, the state of the economy, and beliefs about whether money, fringe benefits, and less tangible forms of remuneration can genuinely motivate employees. Michael Armstrong demonstrates to students how employers:

- evaluate, price, and analyse jobs and roles while ensuring competitiveness and equal pay for work of equal value

- design graded structures, pay spines, and newer broadbanded systems

- integrate reward with performance management

- forge links with individual, team, and corporate results, skills-based pay, competence-based pay, and incentive schemes

- determine the right levels of benefits, allowances, and pensions

- reward directors, executives, expatriates, and sales staff.

Michael Armstrong is one of Britain's best-known authors and an acknowledged authority on reward. He has been closely involved in drafting the Employee Reward module of the new IPD professional standards and is now the chief examiner for this module.

...seems set to become the Wisden of UK employee reward matters...this is the most definitive and up-to-date book [on reward issues] available. Buy.

Duncan Brown, Principal, Towers Perrin

1996 432 pages Paperback ISBN 0 85292 623 5 **£19.95**